MW00397963

A Step-by-Step Guide to Building Your Brand

Why Should you Read this Book?

Create a Personal Brand for YOU

Big companies understand the importance and value of a brand. They develop it, focus on it, pour resources into the marketing and advertising of it, and they reap the benefits of a well-developed and advertised brand. *Think Nike, GE, Quaker, Sony, and Apple.*

Thrive – Don't Just Survive the Changing Times

The world is evolving. Understanding the importance of building a personal brand is a vital step to not only surviving (*layoffs, cutbacks, reductions in force, restructures, buy outs, bosses that don't like you*) but thriving (*promotions, new opportunities, pay raises, new responsibilities, a job you love*).

In this book, I will give you a boost at creating your own personal brand. I will inspire and motivate you with suggestions and ideas that will move you in a positive forward motion. This book will give what you need to create a list of 'To Dos' that when done in easy steps will walk you toward increased profitability and success.

This book will help you to take control of your brand, shape it, and define the brand for YOU or YOUR BUSINESS that will sell and promote you to a market wrought with stiff competition and difficult to acquire positions. It will provide you a career path to enjoyable positions and the best possible pay. This book will help you with critical thinking that can recession-proof your career and your company whether you are an employee seeking to climb in status and position, an entrepreneur seeking to grow your company or an executive running or working in a company. Take the next step toward success. Get reading!

Brand YOU

A Step-by-Step Guide to Building Your Brand

Bethany Williams

Winning Strategies Book 3

ISBN-13: 978-0615502977
ISBN-10: 0615502970

First edition: October 30, 2011

For more information or to contact the author visit:
http://www.BethanyWilliams.org

Printed in the United States of America

Dedication

This book is dedicated to my children, Heather, Brandon and Caleb, and to my loving and supportive husband, Michael. I couldn't write, speak, and conquer the world without their ever-present love and support. Also, to my son-in-law Brian who, with Heather's help, enabled me to have the most adorable grandbaby ever, Madison.

Continued thanks to my supremely supportive parents,, Jim and Elois Eastman of Flint, Michigan, who have loved and supported me throughout my life. Mom and Dad, you are very special to me. I appreciate all that you do.

I feel blessed to be able to have Amy VanVleck, my amazing editor, supporter and friend. She works tirelessly to correct my grammatical errors, re-word sentences that make no sense at all and works diligently to make the book a much better end product.

Many thanks to my continued supporters and fans who have attended my speeches, logged on repeatedly to my web site, emailed and written me, bought my books, and have been the best supporters anyone could have. I hope that I can provide you as much encouragement as you have given me.

Sincerely,

Bethany Williams

Forward

You bought this book because you want to build an incredible brand for yourself that will pay off for you in both compensation and longevity. Reading this book is a great step in the right direction.

Company brands have succeeded, and failed, over the years. We have watched the successes, and known little about the failures. The failures are ripped from the shelves, off into the land of obscurity and we don't hear about them, purchase them, or know of their existence. Have you ever worn a pair of Bic disposable underwear? Me neither, and apparently many others did not either. Yes, Bic really did create disposable underwear. The thought of buying underwear from someone that makes writing utensils didn't turn out to be a successful idea.

Did you serve Colgate Kitchen Entrees for dinner last night? I don't think so. Moms decided quickly that it wasn't a desirable brand for meals that they wanted to feed their family.

Do you drive a Volkswagen Thing or a DeLorean? Both not so popular car brands were attempts at creating a successful brand.

I've read my share of *Cosmopolitan* magazines and they are by many measures one of the most popular magazines of the times. *Cosmopolitan* has 58 international editions, is published in 36 languages and is distributed in more than 100 countries, making it one of the most dynamic brands on the planet. I'd say they have their magazine brand down to a science. All the more reason why it is surprising that they would choose to sell yogurt. Yes, I did say yogurt. From the time of its release, the yogurt was pulled off the shelves within 18 months.

Every component of our lives is touched by brands and branding. We are exposed to information, packaging, and branding on a daily basis. We make decisions and choose purchases based on our knowledge and experience with brands.

You can create a brand that keeps you from being an obscurity. Your brand can be known to those in your company, and even in your industry. You can set a course that will positively brand YOU into a KNOWN entity, place you "in demand" and working a job that you love. This is the time to do it. The pressure of a changing economy makes it the perfect time to create the best brand that will sell you to a market full of competition and constant changes.

Begin your personal climb today.

TABLE OF CONTENTS

CHAPTER 11
Hall of Famers

CHAPTER 10
Being Unique

CHAPTER 9
Hootsuite & Tweetdeck

CHAPTER 8
Facebook & Twitter

CHAPTER 7
LinkedIn & Plaxo

CHAPTER 6
The Google Effect

CHAPTER 5
Advertising Your Brand

CHAPTER 4
The Cornerstones Of Your Brand

CHAPTER 3
Creating Your Brand

CHAPTER 2
How To Define Your Brand

CHAPTER 1
Why Do You Need This?

Chapter 1: Why You Need a Personal Brand

Maybe You've Never Thought of Yourself as a Brand

You may have never thought of yourself as a brand. It may not have crossed your mind. Whether or not you have ever paid any attention to it, you have a distinct brand.

People think of characteristics when they think of you. Something comes to their mind when they think of your work or your business if you are a business leader or owner. The characteristics that come to the top of their mind are the way that they decide whether you are right for a job, whether they select projects or assignments for you, and whether or not they expose you or your business to opportunities.

You are known for something. Your brand may reflect characteristics, attitudes, or adjectives that don't describe you at all. Your brand may be poorly messaged, and may be leading to towards missing opportunities and lost potential. You may never know the opportunities that you have lost as a result of poor personal brand development.

All is not lost. You can assist in the formulation and communication of your brand to provide yourself access to a job, when all others are seeking work. You can put yourself in a situation to grab the positions best suited for you and access to the projects that you would give anything to work on. Your brand can mold and shape the future that you want to be a part of. If you fell into where you are

Brand **YOU**

today, it is not too late to start designing the future that you want to live, not the one you fell into.

Great positions and great jobs don't just happen. Great jobs are the result of great brands and hard work. Great brands are thought out, developed, and carefully crafted and acted on. You make brand decisions every day. You decide what products to buy, what car to drive, what to eat, what to wear, and for which company you want to work. You decide what internet browser to use and whether you want to use a PC or a MAC. Your decisions are based on three things:

- Your perception of the brand
- Whether the brand promise is delivered and
- Your awareness of the brand

Career management isn't covered often enough or thorough enough in the workplace today. Building a personal brand is part of managing your career, your career path, and your earning potential. It will make your work efforts more profitable and more enjoyable. You will have more options presented to you that will allow you to take the paths that you desire if you can develop a sound personal brand that sets you apart in a crowded marketplace. A good brand will open the doors to more opportunities. It will allow you the option to say 'no', if the opportunity isn't right for you.

A good brand is about creating options. It is about you knowing the options that are available. It is about others thinking of you when key positions open and you getting the call. If you are not getting the calls, it is about identifying where you want to go so that you can help others to help you find the opportunities you seek.

You can progressively target a position, role, or career path and make it known that you are interested. If you have an excellent personal brand and work reputation, chances are that you could orchestrate an opportunity that puts you closer to that position.

KEY POINT: **The way that your brand is perceived by others is a deciding factor in whether they select you for a job, pick you for projects or assignments at work, and whether your name is top of mind when opportunities arise.**

If your brand is poorly defined, others will not know how to assist you to achieve. If you can define it, and brand it, you can put yourself in the best possible position to achieve your goals. This book will help you to identify your target goals, determine the audience that can help you get there, and raise the awareness that will assist you in identifying and communicating the areas of your strengths.

I'm already great at what I do. Why would I need a Personal Brand?

You can be fantastic at something, but if the right people don't know how good you are, what have you gained? If there is a position across town for your exact skill set that pays twice what you are making, yet they don't know about you, how would you gain access to that position? What kind of opportunities are you losing out on because of your lack of a personal brand and the inability for others to find you?

It is easy to get comfortable. You really don't want to have to 'work' at anything other than your job. Your brand is worth working on. Should something unforeseen happen, such as a hostile company takeover, an unexpected company bankruptcy, a sudden layoff, new management that brings in their own team, or a reduction in force, you will have a sellable brand with people that know and understand your skill set to fall back on.

Building your brand is like putting money into a savings account. It will pay off if you need it, and if you don't need it, it will still pay off because you will make better decisions without fear immobilizing you. You will have more confidence and will strike out with passion and persistence, relentlessly pursuing your dreams. A great brand will always pay off.

If you aren't great at what you do, then you need to find something to be great at. It will be important to stand out from the crowd and develop differentiating skill sets. Start by thinking of twenty other people that do what you do. What makes you different? What stands out about your capabilities?

❖ ❖ ❖

KEY POINT: It's been said that 'Good things come to those who work.' I'd like to add that good things come to those who BRAND.

I love my job and never want to leave.

You love your job and never want to leave. That is fantastic news. Unfortunately, it may leave you. The technology or product that you work with may become extinct. Think of 35mm film, for example. Eastman Kodak was forced by the digital market to quit making film in 2009 after owning the marketplace for 74 years. They didn't see it coming.

Your company may change all of the leadership. That new leadership team may decide to bring in their own personnel. The company could be acquired or file for bankruptcy. You cannot afford to sit back and hope that all will stay the same indefinitely. The one thing that work can promise you is constant change. You are not guaranteed a job for life. You need to be proactive. Create a brand that will create opportunities for you. Make it so that you possess a brand that makes it easy for you to find another position should the unforeseen happen. Prepare for the unexpected in a similar way that you set aside money in savings to prepare for a rainy day. Your work life is no different. Prepare for unforeseen circumstances with a great brand that allows you to have several options when change does come along – and it will.

The advantage of loving your job is that you can take a slow road to brand development. You are not under the gun or under any pressure to do this quickly. You don't have to rush. You can follow a brand development plan that moves you into brand recognition in three years instead of trying to do it in a year. It simply does not mean that you can ignore personal brand development because you love your job. That could change on a day's notice.

Brand YOU

Do I really need a Personal Brand?

The most common question that I answer via the website and in speeches is 'Do I really need a personal brand?' Whether or not you have a job, branding is about making the most of your earning potential. It is about ensuring that what people think of your work and your achievements reflect good information and show you in the best light possible. The question shouldn't be 'Do I really need a personal brand? You already have one. People think of *something* when they think of you. Today, you may not know what that something is, and it may not fit the direction that you'd like your career or earnings to go.

Developing a personal brand allows you to take control of your brand and mold and shape it to fit the brand and message that you want to communicate. The perception of your work and who you are is the basis for your earnings and your earning potential, whether or not you take control of it. You care about your personal brand development if you want to achieve the most that you can achieve and utilize your skill sets and gifts to their maximum potential and reward.

KEY POINT: You are in charge of brand management, marketing, sales, customer support, and collateral development for your brand. You own it. You are ultimately responsible for it and you will reap the financial benefits of a well-developed brand.

A well-developed personal brand can help you to focus. You can easily get busy and lose track of your destination. You can get lost in the shuffle and forget your ultimate destination. A documented brand will help you to stay the course throughout the years. It can help you to maintain focus in your career journey and stay on a consistent course. It will be your road map toward your chosen career or the development of your business.

You want to think of yourself as a brand because of the money you can make with personal brand development. You will make more money. I am referring to salary, hourly rate increases, bonuses, pay increases, business deals, and stock options. You will spend X number of years working. In those years, you will work to attain a position that you enjoy and something, you hope, that you do well. If you find what you do well, you will attempt to maximize the income that you can make out of your skills. You will do this by developing a personal brand that stands for what you do well and an outline for the path that you would like to take.

Opportunities Abound

Chances are good that someone that you know or are somehow connected to is looking to fill a position. They may or may not have thought of you for that position. What makes you a great accountant, business manager, health care leader, secretary, consultant, intern, or X? If you have a business, what makes your services valuable to others? What makes you stand out and create for them the thought that they should contact you for the position or to buy your services or send you a contract? It is your brand.

Brand **YOU**

Your brand is what they think of when they think of you.
Brands can be negative and/or positive. If you haven't
thought through the planning of it, you could be creating a
negative brand without even realizing it. This book will
help you take control of your brand, shape it, and define the
brand that can provide you a career path to enjoyable
positions and the best pay. You can create a brand that will
package and sell yourself or your services to the market. It
can help you with critical thinking that can recession-proof
your career.

Your Brand Elements

You buy products and services because of what you believe
about them. You have created an image in your mind of
the characteristics that you can expect from the brands that
you buy. The same thoughts that you have about buying
products and services apply to your personal brand. Start
by thinking through these three brand components:

- What would you define your brand to be? How do
  you want to be known? We will cover this in detail
  in Chapter 2.
- How will you raise awareness of your personal
  brand? How will you market and 'live' your brand?
  We will cover this in Chapters 3 through 9.
- How will you ensure that you deliver on your brand
  promise? We will cover this in Chapter 10.

Your Brand Today: Outside-in View

Let's begin. We will start with a little homework. Locate
five people that you either work with today or have worked
with in the past.

Give them the following questions via email or phone. Ask them to kindly answer honestly, since you are working on a career path planning exercise and their answers and honesty are critical to the success of the exercise. Tell them that you will not be contentious or upset with them over their honesty. You need honest constructive criticism for this to be a successful exercise.

Dear _____,

Thank you for agreeing to assist me in my career path planning exercise. I need your honest input on the following three questions. This will help me to define a path forward and will give me a chance to understand both the positive and any negative aspects that you think of when you think of my work skills and experiences.

1) I can always count on (insert your name) to:

    _____

2) When I think of your work skills, what really stands out is your ability to:

    _____

    _____

3) Characteristics that I think of when I think about you and your work are:

    a. Positive:_____

Brand YOU

_____

b. Negative:_____

_____

Thank you!

****

This homework is vitally important. In fact, it alone was worth the price of this book. This critical information will help you to understand how people perceive you or your business today. It will also help you to understand positive traits that are reflected in your work. You will want to accentuate the positive and avoid brand statements that point to your negative characteristics. If you understand the positive characteristics that you possess, you can use those to capitalize on the positions and opportunities that maximize those assets. You can embrace the parts of you that are you.

Your Brand Today: Inside-out View

Your homework also includes your own view of how you are perceived in the workplace and on the projects that you work on. Time is of the essence. How are you spending your time? Are you productive at work? How are you perceived in the meetings that you attend? Are they productive? Are your projects completed on time and done well? If you are in sales, how promptly do you follow up? For leaders, do your employees love and respect you or shy away in fear when you walk by?

Carefully scrutinize your own work. Evaluate the work you do as if you were the owner of the company. Take a very critical eye to your attitude, your own work, and the relationships that you have or haven't formed with your co-workers, boss, and subordinates. Do you build others up? Do you ignite a positive, get-it-done attitude that permeates all of those around you to want to perform better, work harder, and be at the top of their game? Or, on the other hand, are you dragging others down and pulling down the office productivity? Are you liked or disliked at work? Are you achieving the goals set for you? What do your employment reviews say?

How do you look and dress? Do you carry yourself well? Does your look complement the company or do you drag down the standards? If you have trouble with this inside-out assessment, you could always call your mother, sister, brother or another relative. Relatives often tell us the honest to goodness truth when others might tell a boldface lie. Ask someone at work that doesn't like you or someone who recently quit to answer these questions; they may be more honest with you. Write down the adjectives that come to mind. Make a list of what you think you do very well and areas where you need to improve. Stop thinking 'Why do I care?' and move toward 'I care and aim to improve.' This shift will be noticeable at work and will improve your value and brand positioning.

Your Strengths Play Into Your Brand

The strengths that you possess will help to form your brand. You have been born with strengths. These strengths will help you to stand out from others in the same profession or with the same skill set. You are uniquely gifted with innate strengths.

If you haven't yet deciphered your strengths, try thinking about the things that you enjoy doing the most. You are energized when you use your strengths. You won't tire of doing these things. They are things that you love to do. If you truly had a job using many of your strengths, it would be a job that you would greatly enjoy, you would do it very well, and others would see you as very successful at it. Your goal is to understand your strengths so well that you use them to define your brand, and strive to move into a position that uses your strengths on a daily basis.

Competition from others becomes less noticeable when you are utilizing your strengths. You have been born with gifts in these areas. As you find these strengths, using them will make you stand out from others seeking the same positions. You will excel.

There are online resources and books to help identify strengths. Author Marcus Buckingham has several books regarding identifying and finding your strengths. Some of the titles include *Now, Discover Your Strengths*, *Strengthsfinder 2.0*, and *The Truth About You*. Each book comes with a code to log into an online assessment tool that will help you to identify your strengths. Find it on the web at www.strengthsfinder.com. Strengths are not learned. They are innate. They are inborn, natural and instinctive. Like the seeds in a watermelon, they have been placed within you from the beginning of your life. They make you distinct. You are unique and different from anyone else, born with special skills that will help you to stand apart in a crowd.

Knowing what makes you tick and understanding your unique gifts is extremely important in developing your personal brand and will ultimately help you to achieve the most success you can achieve in your career journey. The most important goal is self-exploration to identify these key strengths.

What activities/tasks do I enjoy doing?

1) _____

2) _____

3) _____

4) _____

5) _____

What are the characteristics/similarities of these activities?

1) _____

2) _____

3) _____

4) _____

5) _____

Brand YOU

What are my common themes/strengths?

1)_____

2) _____

3) _____

4) _____

5) _____

Strive to keep working at strength identification until you have perfected it. It is worth the time to explore and develop this key component of who you are. Learning to understand this piece about yourself will help you to achieve, succeed, and arrive where you want to go.

The Vital Importance of Building Your Personal Brand

Building your personal brand is going to be easier than you think. This book contains a list of 'To Dos' that, when broken down into small pieces, don't have to be overwhelming. Pick out items that you can accomplish and plot them onto your calendar over the next 12-36 months. Each chapter will summarize those tasks for you. Assign tasks over a broad time period. Develop a plan to form your personal brand and catapult yourself forward. You can push yourself and/or your company toward success.

Personal Brand "To Do" List

Chapter 1: Why Do You Need This?
- Locate five people to assess your work and what YOU stand for
- Evaluate YOUR view of your work
- Identify your strengths

CHAPTER 11
Hall of Famers

CHAPTER 10
Being Unique

CHAPTER 9
Hootsuite & Tweetdeck

CHAPTER 8
Facebook & Twitter

CHAPTER 7
LinkedIn & Plaxo

CHAPTER 6
The Google Effect

CHAPTER 5
Advertising Your Brand

CHAPTER 4
The Cornerstones Of Your Brand

CHAPTER 3
Creating Your Brand

CHAPTER 2
How To Define Your Brand

CHAPTER 1
Why Do You Need This?

Chapter 2: Defining Your Brand

Who are you?

The best way to begin defining your brand is to ask yourself, "Who am I?" "What do I stand for?" "What makes me unique and different?"

In this exercise, you will not differentiate your personal traits from your work traits. Personal traits can differentiate you. If you are personable or gregarious, it can help you define your personal brand. Work to make your personal traits a positive part of your brand.

Who do you want to be?

If you worked your dream job, what would it entail? Have you spent time pondering this? Concentrate on the characteristics of the positions that you desire. I clearly remember sitting in the back of a room at my place of employment, watching a software demonstration. I was early into my career as a hospital administrator. I was thinking how fun it would be to be speaking to groups of people. Have you ever had a thought like that? Have you seen a position or witnessed someone in a particular job that made you stop and think, "How fun would that be?" After identifying the strengths that you possess in Chapter 1, which of those tasks and strengths would you like to use in your job?

Only 20% of people in positions today are working in their strengths area. This is a horrendously sad fact. Why would you want to spend 50 years doing something that you don't

18

enjoy? Eighty percent of workers are doing the job that they just happened upon and stayed in because it was easy, necessary or convenient. They are not defining what they want to do or striving to get into a position that uses their strengths and points them toward a future that better defines who they are and what they want to become. Are you one of those people? Don't let yourself get stuck in this position endlessly.

Never stop striving toward what you want to be and do. You are driving the bus that is your career path and life journey.

Perspective and Positive Attitude

One of the best ways to define and shape your brand is to form it around a positive global perspective. These are great traits to add to your brand. When you are complaining about your job or company, you are fogging up the picture and making it hard to define a good brand and move forward. You are in control. You are defining your goals and how you will advance.

Your assignment is to find a global and far-reaching perspective. This perspective needs to take into consideration the slanted views that you may be projecting on the canvas of your mind. Your goal is to open up the shudders and create a realistic ruler with which to measure your world and the world around you. Consider donating some of your time and efforts to a charitable organization. Spend a day at the homeless shelter. Work in the closest soup kitchen. Volunteer at a local charity. This time will be well spent. Consider visiting a Third World country or watching a video of life in a Third World country. Your goal is to walk away with a wider perspective. Your goal is to attempt to see your world through different glasses. You are attempting to see how you can stand tall and make a difference, savoring each little gift that life has given you in the past and has in store for you in the future.

The purpose of this suggestion is to help you broaden the camera angles. You are to begin seeing what your world can be rather than solely concentrating on what it is and what it is not. This new reality perspective is vital in the beginning phases of personal brand development. You have to wipe the slate clean. You are to shape and mold a perspective that says that you will begin to see the world around you from its possibilities rather than its inabilities or limitations. You are to begin the process by opening up your eyes to a global economy and the realities of your current situation that you may be taking for granted.

You will need this positive perspective to form your brand. A professor once asked me to stay after class. It was a computer programming class and I was fearful that I had flunked the final. He explained that the code that I had written showed great talent in programming (who knew?). I was perplexed; I had taken the longest to complete the final exam. He said the quality of my programming code far exceeded all others in the class. I thought I had failed. My perspective was off. Find that positive perspective with regard to your work. Find what differentiates you. Look for qualities that bosses seek. It may take you a little longer to do something, but are you more accurate than anyone else on the team? You may spend more time in preparation for the project, but have all your projects come in on time and on budget? Look for positive aspects of your work that have paid off for you and your employers

over time. These will be vital in defining your brand.
What my professor saw as amazing, I had seen as complete
failure. Redefine your greatness. Find the jewels hidden
within.

A second component to positivity is to clearly see the best
possible result in all situations. This quality is lacking in
many laboring away in companies today. Positive teams
accomplish more. They are more productive. Positivity
breeds more positivity. It multiplies across the employees.
If you can accomplish a positive attitude, it can become one
of the assets in your brand library.

**KEY POINT: If you can accomplish a positive attitude,
it could become one of the assets in your brand library.**

How to Make Your Brand Uniquely You

Your brand is about you. It is about the uniqueness of you.
It cannot be mundane or expected. Someone once
suggested that her brand was dependability. She was
applying for a highly compensated accounting position.
Dependability in that role is expected. It is not a brand
quality that will set her apart from the others applying for
that same role. Dependability in a retail clerk position
could be considered a valuable asset. As you define your
personal brand, consider the role and the compensation
range and the uniqueness of your personality and traits.

Remember, you are working to design a brand and image that will occupy a distinctive place in the mind of others and set you apart from your peers. This brand needs to open doors to new opportunities, new positions and, potentially, to a new path for you. You cannot do that with expected or mundane assets.

Take the strengths that you identified in Chapter 1. Write them down.

What are your identified strengths?

1)

2)

3)

4)

5)

Think about your proudest accomplishments. What characteristics did those entail? What did you do to achieve those results?

I believe that the customer is the key to success. They, in effect, buy what you are selling. Some corporate cultures get wrapped up in a less-than customer-first attitude. I decided early on that I would ensure that my customers knew how I felt about meeting their needs and providing them with amazing service. I would walk through walls to make sure that their needs were met. They knew it. They could sense it. As a leader in a software company, they knew I'd make sure that their needs were met and we met our commitments. One customer once asked in a contract for a 'what if Bethany quits?' clause. I knew at that point that I had created value for the customer. He knew that as long as I was employed, commitments would be kept and his organization would be taken care of. If I left the company, he had concerns that his organization's needs may not be kept and he wanted an option to renegotiate if that situation occurred. What value and brand are you building in your organization?

What are the top three characteristics reflected in your proudest accomplishments?

1)

2)

3)

Now think about the position that you have or the one that you desire to have. What characteristics would make you shine in that position?

Then ask yourself: What are the top three desirable characteristics for my desired or current role?

1)

2)

3)

Work the above into sentences. These are your brand statements. This is the beginning of the formation of your written brand.

KEY POINT: You are working to design a brand and image that will occupy a distinctive place in the mind of others.

A Sample Brand

There was a point in my career journey that I felt that not having a clear way to differentiate my skills from the skills of others was holding me back. I felt that I was not being offered the best positions, the best assignments, and was not being called to interview for the 'hottest' opportunities as they were dreamed up, even before they were posted, therefore preventing me from financially living up to my potential.

What made me different from every other business executive out there? How could I substantiate additional responsibilities and pay if I couldn't communicate and clearly deliver a brand value? I decided to develop a brand and see if it created financial and position-oriented benefits. I couldn't have been more satisfied with the results. The results of a well-developed brand paid off far more than I had ever imagined it would. I began to get five to seven calls a week from companies looking for my skill set. I couldn't answer all the calls that came in. I began to interview two or three times a year to understand the evolving market and keep an eye on the horizon should things ever change at work.

I became exposed to new opportunities before they were fully developed. I had opportunity to help create positions designed just for me. I was defining my future. It was more than I expected from brand creation. You will be amazed at what you can achieve with a well-developed brand.

I define my brand as 'a business leader with business development skills,' a 'rainmaker.' I came up with 'rainmaker' because several of the interviews that I did with professionals that I have worked with contained that phraseology. People think of 'rainmaker' when they think of me. Since it is a trait that fits the positions that I want to hold, I added it to my brand statement. They also commented on 'results oriented' and 'motivated/ motivational.' I am targeted for positions where companies are looking to grow into a new market share, add divisions or departments, and then potentially IPO or sell the business. I am consistently sought after for new market growth areas.

I added some of my strengths to the key words that came out of the interviews and a list began to take shape:

- Business leader
- Rainmaker
- High integrity
- Results-oriented executive with the ability to get things done
- Creating business units and new market strategies to grow market share

- Out-of-the-box thinker
- Gifted speaker and communicator

To further delineate me from the others, I added four more components to my brand:

- Networked professional
- Problem solver
- Supportive/passionate about women and diversity initiatives
- Passionate about helping executives to live their best lives

The four additional components that I added to my brand were not a part of my existing persona or brand, but I had a desire for them to become part of my brand. They didn't describe me at that time. Although I had that inclination, I hadn't allowed it to show up at work. Those four remaining components described who I wanted to be at work.

Pick components that embody who you are and who you'd like to be. These unique components will help you to stand apart from the others. Add passions into the mix. Have you lost a loved one to cancer? Do you have a passion for the American Heart Association? Are you interested in the Girl Scouts or Boy Scouts? Ross Perot Sr. has a passion for veterans. His passion is incorporated into companies where he works and where he invests his money. What is your passion? Be who you were destined to be. Be passionate about a cause and work it into your brand. It is a part of who you are. Embrace it.

Brand **YOU**

KEY POINT: When defining your brand, pick components that embody who you are and who you'd like to be. These unique components will help you to define your brand and stand apart from the crowd.

◆ ◆ ◆

One CEO that I dealt with had a brand of 'doing the right thing.' He was amazingly successful because of it. His brand played out in the way that he worked and in the decisions that he made. Even if the contract didn't require the work to be done, he would authorize it if it was the right thing to do for the customer.

Once, the company had missed giving me a bonus that I had earned. When I was ready to leave the company, I mentioned the missed bonus in a conversation with the CEO. I figured that I had nothing to lose on my way out the door. He promised to pay me for the bonus whether I stayed or left the firm. He wanted to do the right thing regardless of whether it was going to pay off for the company. The attitude and brand that he developed followed suit. He paid me for the bonus even though he was expecting me to leave the company. Because of the brand that he represented, and the way he ran the company, I stayed. It was a brand that I wanted to be a part of.

Differentiate Yourself

Imagine hundreds, if not thousands of people looking for the same positions that you want. What would make you stand out from the crowd? What could differentiate your skill set from the thousands of others? What makes you different? It is not unusual for companies today to get more than 1,000 resumes for posted position. Think about how hard it will be for you to stand out against those kinds of odds.

This is the time to go on a journey of discovery. It is important to understand that, from elementary school to now, there are tasks that you've excelled at doing. I greatly admire Ross Perot,Sr. I worked for him for a period of time and loved the way that he had his recruiters look for new employees. He wants to find employees that have excelled at something since elementary school. He wants to find the best of the best. He coaches his recruiters to find needles in haystacks that have little red dots on them. He wants only the select few. His strategy works. He continually finds amazingly talented resources that have helped him to build two large companies in his lifetime. His first company, Electronic Data Systems (EDS), was sold to General Motors in 1984 for 2.5 billion dollars. He then started Perot Systems Corporation in June of 1988 and sold it to Dell in September 2009 for 3.9 billion dollars. His ability to select talented resources to grow his companies is obviously off-the-charts amazing. It is rare to find a businessman as remarkably successful and talented as Ross Perot,Sr.

You, too, excel at something. You need to find it and incorporate that into your brand. Once you have identified 'what' you want to market about yourself, this book will walk you through the next steps on 'how to' package your message, publicize, and live your brand.

Brand YOU

KEY POINT: From elementary school to now, it is important to understand and identify anything that you have excelled at doing.

Did you sell magazines door to door indicating you're a natural-born salesman? Were you class president in high school indicating you are a natural-born leader? What were your natural inclinations and what skills do they point to?

As you work through the chapters of this book, you are moving through the steps of defining how you want to differentiate yourself as well as identifying components that you won't want to be a part of your brand. Branding is about what you stand for, what you are, and what you are not.

The Value of the Brand

What if when you woke up this morning and were awarded the rights to the brand for Crest Toothpaste or General Electric? You would be wealthy. Both brands have intrinsic value in and of themselves. They have created goodwill and trust elements in their brands that make them valuable. They are worth millions, if not billions in brand value alone.

You are the CEO and owner of Brand YOU _____ (insert your name here). You can benefit from your brand worth. You can market, message and capitalize on your brand. You own the rights and all profits made from your brand. If you brand yourself, your services, or your company well, you could increase your job security, job options, and your annual salary or worth. It is shocking to think about the number of hours that you may have spent in college or business school compared to how little time you have probably spent developing the messaging and components of your career compass that translate into your salary and worth.

The value of your brand is a valuable asset. Ask Bill Gates if he thinks a brand has value. I would wager a bet that he would say a resounding 'Yes!' The company doesn't 'own you.' You are in charge of your career path, your career, your brand, your ultimate destination, and the enjoyment that you do [or do not] derive from your job. Now is the time to figure out your strengths, the personal traits that make you different, and how you stand apart from the others so you can create a valuable brand that will catapult you forward. Pause for a moment and think through this section. Doing this now will increase your worth and your job security, safely and comfortably landing in a position you like and generally enjoy. Don't put this off any longer. This is the time.

If you had tried to convince me of this six years ago, I wouldn't have believed you. What has changed, you ask? I have seen the benefit of developing a valuable brand. I have witnessed the options and salary increases that come with a great brand. I have helped countless others develop valuable brands that have cemented their worth, created job offers and pay raises for them and helped them to arrive at new and exciting destinations. I have helped businesses develop brand that have catapulted them to the top of their industries. Brands pay off. Can you afford to not brand yourself? Wouldn't it be worth the effort to try?

KEY POINT: The company doesn't 'own you.' You are in charge of your career path, your career, your brand, your ultimate destination, and the enjoyment that you do or do not derive from your job.

Don't Forget the Packaging

You buy certain foods and products based on the packaging. You must think about your packaging, too. What image do you project? Would you buy a carton of pudding or yogurt if it was smashed, crinkled, or bent out of shape? Is your brand crinkled or bent out of shape? Has your attitude been smashed or crushed into something that doesn't reflect who you are?

Successful people really do present themselves differently. They look pulled together. They represent an image that instills confidence that allows you to believe that they will be able to get the job done. They are attentive to detail. They are able to present themselves professionally with a look that says, "I can do it." Success dresses differently.

Don't let your appearance hide the brilliance beneath. Your image is part of your brand. The way you look can either move you up the ladder to success or hold you down. Recognize that both your skills and your image will work together to build your brand and catapult or restrict your road to success. A well-developed and thought-through image will increase your chances for being more marketable.

Product companies understand this. They redo their product's packaging when sales drop. They know that changing the outside packaging without doing anything to the content or actual product can positively impact their sales. If it works for them, it could work for you.

'Looking the part' is part of your brand packaging. Your image makes up a component of your brand. What could you consider that would improve your image and potentially better promote you in your industry? It could be the way you dress, the technology or tools that you use at the office, or even your office and desk can reflect on your image and brand.

How often to do you think through this component of your identity and brand? Often we think through this in detail when we are suddenly forced to look for work. Don't wait for that situation to evaluate, assess and create the 'best of you' action plan.

Consider adding components to your lifestyle that include eating healthy and exercising. Eating right, exercising, and staying youthful and vibrant, or keeping a young look as best you can is a great prescription for your life, isn't it? It will give you a chance at a longer career in your new healthier body.

You leave behind a sign that tells others that you are either heading for success, already arrived, or not heading for success at all. A body or look that hasn't been cared for and is sloppy or unprofessional can inhibit your brand and keep you from opportunities.

Packaging Includes a Logo and a Catch Phrase

Packaging includes a logo, pictures, designs and a catch phrase. AT&T had a phrase, *'Rethink Possible.'* You know brands that you've come to know and love based on the logos that they've created to help you identify their brands.

Create a logo for yourself. Create a phrase that describes you and who you are. What is your business motto? What is your personal motto? Create a logo and a catch phrase that seeks to catch the attention of others. This may sound crazy. Accept that this will help you to visualize your brand. It will help you to identify the components of YOU that are different.

My business motto: Put people and their needs ahead of business needs through servant leadership and acting with character and integrity.

My personal motto: Motivating and inspiring you to live your best life.

Create a business motto for yourself:

_____

_____

Create a personal motto for yourself:

_____

_____

Well done! The journey has begun. You will achieve more by beginning to define the map, the direction you are heading, and the path to get there.

Read on for ideas on messaging the brand that you've created. Brands, once developed, are publicized, advertised, and enforced.

Personal Brand "To Do" List

Chapter 2: How to Define Your Brand
o   Identify what you want to be known for
o   Document your strengths
o   Write out the top three characteristics
    reflected in your proudest accomplishments
o   Write out three desired characteristics for
    your desired or current role
o   Create a logo and a catch phrase

Bethany Williams

Chapter 3: Creating the YOU Brand

Your Message

Companies have goals and objectives. Annually they publish what they stand for and what they hope to accomplish. They announce the 'pillars' of value and where they will focus their attention. It is short and sweet. It is simply stated and explains what they are trying to accomplish. You will publish your brand message. You will write it up and communicate verbally how you will be making a difference in your position and your company. You will begin to define your road map to success the same way that the companies all around us do.

It will sound like an advertisement for you. It will signify the brand that you have identified as *your* brand. If you can't write an advertisement for yourself, then why would you be so cruel as to accept a paycheck from your employer? Accept that you have value. Verbalize it. Write it down and document it.

Your goal is to know your brand and use it as a compass to guide you toward your goals and, ultimately, in the direction that you want your work life to go. What do you want to be? How do you want to be known? How can you distinctly use your strengths and personal characteristics to message yourself?

Start simple.

I am _____, _____, _____
(insert characteristics that came out in the interviews that you conducted about yourself)

Brand **YOU**

with a passion and a desire to
_____
(What do you want to be/do? What position do you want to have?)

My core strengths are:

    1)_____

    2)_____

    3)_____

    4)_____

    5)_____

I am especially gifted at:_____
(Insert a distinguishing trait that helps you to stand out.)

This may be difficult if you don't already have a professional biography. If you don't have one, let's start with creating a biography.

A biography is a great tool to record and document your career progress as you move up the ladder. A biography gives a work history for you. It tells the reader why you are 'worthy.'   No matter how many of these you have or haven't written you may not always feel like you are worthy. Your goal is to believe in yourself and have bold confidence even before you have a long list of companies that you have worked for or even despite being unemployed for a long period. If you have experience, and you haven't yet written one or revised yours in some time,

Bethany Williams

start here. Write one now. Before you do one more thing today, write a quick and easy, new or updated bio. If yours is outdated, update it now.

Your Biography

BIOGRAPHY

_____(your name) is the

_____(title of your current job) at

_____(company you work for)

working to _____.
(standard company goal or business statement of purpose)

Prior to his current role at _____,
                                                (company)
_____ was _____
(last name)   (title and job description)

_____.

_____(last name) received his/her

_____(name of degree) in

_____(specialty) from

_____(university).

Congratulations! This is a great start. Now I suggest you write a bio that reflects where you would like to be in one

38

to seven years from now. Picture your bio as you progress on your career track. Use it as a motivational tool to visualize your successful career path and your journey.

Once you've edited or created your bio, you can use that as a catapult to your personal brand. You can now begin to mold and shape the message that will bring out your distinctive characteristics.

We will now move onward to the development of your brand. It could have a variety of aspects:

Aspects of Your Brand

- **Trade or skills:**
  How would you classify your trade or skills? Would you call yourself a great accountant, a viable leader, a decision support analyst, a designer extraordinaire, etc? Find words that pop and leave a lasting impression.
- **Special skills:**
  Differentiate yourself from others doing the same thing that you do by finding components that you have focused on or specialized in. If you don't have any of these components today, map out a plan to create a focus and identify some. Every field has credentials you can seek out or expertise that you could define or specialize in.
- **YOU:**
  Your brand is about you. Be prepared to locate pieces of your personality or specific characteristics that define you and make you who you are. How would your best cheerleader describe you?

- **Interests:**
  Find sector or special areas that are of interest to you. Maybe they would sound something like creating amazing client experiences, productivity genius, project supporter, visionary, thought leader, diversity proponent, 'go green' advocate, supply chain efficiencies, solar power interests, etc. What special interest do you have personally that could benefit your employer (or yourself if you are self-employed)? Embrace all aspects of your interests and desires.

Communicate It

Once you have defined your brand, then let's move on to communicating your brand. Defining your brand and what you want to be known for is often the most difficult part. Whew, now that you have accomplished that component, the easier work begins. Now, how will you communicate your personal brand?

You can communicate your brand in several ways:

1. Your actions
2. Your reactions
3. The way you package yourself
4. The way you express yourself in both verbal and written communications

Your Actions

When you have defined your brand, it becomes the compass by which you can point your legs. It is the direction that you know you want to go. Success or greater job satisfaction is at the other end of that defined path and you will march toward it. Your actions will then reinforce your brand. If you've defined your brand as a 'productive and efficient worker,' then your actions will need to coincide with that brand statement.

If you've defined a brand of 'leadership' then you will need actions that lead. The best leaders lead by example. So if you want to be known as a great leader, yet you work the least, take the longest lunches, don't speak well in meetings, and don't efficiently accomplish your workload, then you really won't have a brand of 'leadership.' I get many emails from those of you that do have leaders like that. Remember, that this is a marathon, not a foot race. The true winners will be the ones that combine a great brand with great performance over a long period of time. Do not get discouraged by the co-workers that say one thing and march to a different beat.

It is imperative that your actions match up to your brand. Many a sports professional or actor has had this dilemma. Every actor and talent in the industry defines a brand. They use that brand to sell sponsorships, advertisements, and to make additional monies from the other things that they do. Many of those brands are none too happy when the actor or sports figure steps outside of their brand and delivers a message *through their actions* that reflects poorly on the brand. There are many examples of people stepping outside of the brands that they created: Tiger Woods creating a stir with antics in his marriage; Madonna creating children's books after developing a wild playgirl brand and a book titled 'Sex' with eye-popping nude photos, just to name a couple. The list could go on and on.

As you read this, relatives and college roommates come to mind that match the pattern.

Your actions are the loudest statement about your brand aspirations. They will speak louder than anything else that you do.

I once talked to an interviewer who said that she never hired sales people that didn't go in for the close. She said, "How can I expect them to close business if they can't even close the interview and ask for the position?" She has a good point. Do your actions line up with your brand statement? Are you reflecting to others the message that you want to send?

Think of yourself as a professional sports figure or an actor/actress. It is a good way to position the thought process. Who they are is greatly critiqued. If they reflect the 'family' image, yet are caught out partying with a group of people, using drugs and abusing alcohol, then the image of them is taken from their actions.

Your actions will speak for you. Either they will be in sync with the brand that you'd like to reflect to others or they will be in stark contrast to what you want your brand to be. Decide what you want your brand to be and be cautiously aware that the message that will go out will be based on your actions, not on how you have defined your brand.

Your Reactions

We want to be known as compassionate, but then we laugh at someone being ridiculed at work. We want to be trusted and respected, but then we sit quietly listening to a coworker talk badly about our boss. We want to be known as efficient and productive, but then we spend an inordinate amount of time gossiping or chit-chatting about sports at a coworker's desk.

Your reactions and the conversations that you have will speak loudly of your brand and who you are. As CEO of Brand YOU, you are not only responsible to define your brand, but you also must:

- Market
- Sell
- Communicate &
- Plan

You are in charge of brand management, marketing, sales, customer support, and collateral development for your brand. You own it. You are ultimately responsible for it. You will reap the benefits of a well-developed brand.

The Way You Package Yourself or Your Company

If you want to quickly redirect and revive a worn out brand, redesign the packaging. Re-tool your image. Buy new clothes. Schedule a professional photography appointment to get a great head shot to accompany your bio or descriptions of what you do for your company. Order a new nametag. Buy a new pen and notepad that reflect the image that you'd like to project. Review magazines and advertisements selecting one or two images that best reflect the look that you'd like to attain. Replace that worn out briefcase, tool belt, or other key ingredient in your workday. Upgrade your electronics. Straighten up the mess that you call a desk or the inside of your truck, delivery van, taxicab or front office. These things really do matter. They speak to the image that others have of you.

◆ ◆ ◆

KEY POINT: You are in charge of brand management, marketing, sales, customer support, and collateral development for your brand. You own it. You are ultimately responsible for it.

◆ ◆ ◆

Look closely at your image. Look at your total image. How do you present the 'product' that you create? What is displayed on your business cards? If you are self-employed, do your business cards and collateral pieces look professional and SCREAM success? Are they unique? If there were 100 cards on a desktop, would yours stand out? Do you have a logo and a catchy phrase?

If you are an early careerist, are you dressing for the level where you want to arrive, or lazily wearing whatever because you think it doesn't really matter yet?

It does matter. The compilation of these little things adds up to create a component of your brand. You can impact what others think of YOU or YOUR BUSINESS in many distinct ways.

Go to a food court where crowds of executives congregate. Sit down for two hours and watch the people pass by. Try to guess their position, level of income and type of company. What do you see? Does it surprise you how

Brand YOU

much you can figure out from just watching? What are people figuring out from watching you? Is this limiting you or helping you find the job of your dreams?

Expressing Yourself Through Communication

Communication is a constant component of your work life, offering continual opportunity to impact your brand and re-state who you are and what you or your business stands for. In this rushed world, often communication is poorly written and delivered. Often we succumb to electronic communications when verbal or in-person communication would have been a much better option.

You rush through write-ups and deliver reports and finished products that are a poor reflection of your brand and image. You halfway do things and create a less than fabulous result that is documented and distributed for all to see. You don't give it another thought because you are busy, hurried, and on to the next assignment or task. Every written or verbal communication is a reflection of who you are and who you aim to be. Make each one great!

Your Work Product and the Results You Achieve

Your goal should be 100% out-of-this-world work. Your goal should be to achieve the most incredible results possible. It should cause people to want to talk about YOU or YOUR COMPANY and the results that you achieve. You are working toward the 'buzz factor.' You are working to STAND OUT.

What you produce, how you do it, and the results you achieve are part of YOU (aka, your brand). It is sometimes shocking that this component isn't 100% of your brand. It is a component, however a very large component, of who you are at work. It will form the basis, the core infrastructure, of your brand. Aspects of this should be reflected in the brand interviews you conducted. If no one commented on your work results, you have to ask yourself this question: is it because I didn't achieve notable results or because I did a poor job of marketing and touting the results that I achieved? Creating a brand about results is two-fold:

- Create the results
- Advertise the results

Write up an advertisement with two to three great results that you achieved this year. Start thinking about how regularly you should advertise. What messages would you think valuable to deliver? As marketing manager for Brand YOU, you will decide how often to advertise your accomplishments.

One hundred percent of successful people have figured out self-promotion. And you know what they have accomplished. You know what they do well. You know what they stand for. You know because they've told you. And because employers know what they can do, doors of opportunity open for them. What doors may open for you when you begin to advertise and tout your capabilities? What are the top five accomplishments of your entire career to date? Are they written anywhere? Are they advertised? Do people that know you, know what you have achieved? Could they advertise for you if an opportunity came up?

❖   ❖   ❖

KEY POINT: What you produce, how you do it, and the results you achieve are part of Brand YOU. Tout it!

❖   ❖   ❖

I had a business contact that I'd known and worked with for some time. Even after knowing her for more than three years, I was shocked to discover that she had received a business development 'heavy hitter' award several years back from a prominent business journal in the area. Despite our many conversations, it had never come up. It was also information that was buried in her LinkedIn profile, and not easy to spot. It kept me from adequately 'advertising' her capabilities and describing her capabilities when I referred her for a business development role. Don't be shy about advertising your capabilities. Aid your network in their ability to support and advertise for you by giving them ammunition to use when opportunities arise for which you would be an excellent candidate.

I have spent years of my life in the consulting field. Consulting is about expertise. It is about specialties. It is about brand. People hire consultants because of what they know, the accomplishments they've achieved and the experience that they can bring to the table. I am amazed day after day at the number of experts in any given field that have never fully developed their brand or advertised their capabilities. What are they losing? They are losing out on opportunities, billable work, people seeking them out and easily finding them, and discussions that would lead to billable work (i.e., a consultants' best friend).

Enforcing your brand through your web presence, social media, and emails sent throughout your company, and other modes will be discussed in the next chapter.

Personal Brand "To Do" List

Chapter 3: Creating Your Brand
o Create a message for your brand
o Write or update your biography
o Begin to think about communicating your brand
o Re-tool your image

CHAPTER 11
Hall of Famers

CHAPTER 10
Being Unique

CHAPTER 9
Hootsuite & Tweetdeck

CHAPTER 8
Facebook & Twitter

CHAPTER 7
LinkedIn & Plaxo

CHAPTER 6
The Google Effect

CHAPTER 5
Advertising Your Brand

CHAPTER 4
The Cornerstones Of Your Brand

CHAPTER 3
Creating Your Brand

CHAPTER 2
How To Define Your Brand

CHAPTER 1
Why Do You Need This?

Chapter 4: The Cornerstones of the YOU Brand

Within every corporate branding statement is a list of values and cornerstones that drive the decision making and core direction that the company takes. Your brand should encompass the key values that are uniquely you. These values define you. They are a key part of who you are. Your family values, core belief system, the way you think, the work ethic that you have, and the virtues that you posses all should be carefully considered in the construction of the YOU brand.

For which values and virtues do you want to be known? What values best describe you? Write them down. They are components that you can use in the development of your brand. You should start seeing a distinctive road map, a picture of you in words that looks entirely different from anyone you know. You are distinct. You possess a unique set of values, skills, and talents that are marketable and differentiate you from the thousands of others seeking the same roles or pursuing similar futures. They are your key to standing out in a sea of people in this super-competitive landscape surrounding you and your next opportunity.

Be True to Yourself

Your true colors shine whether you desire them to or not. We see evidence of this daily in Hollywood when an actor is caught in an activity 'outside their brand.' If you are a family man, I advise that you not pretend to be a hard-core partygoer and vice-versa. Don't fall into the trap of believing that companies want you to pretend to be

Brand YOU

something that you are not just to fit in. Leave that attitude back in high school where it belongs. You do not have to pretend to be someone else to get a pay raise or that next-level promotion. Your goal is to find the company that allows you to be YOU, not try to fit yourself into a culture or brand that doesn't fit you. Companies and executives alike respect people that are true to who they are. Honesty in the depiction of your brand is important. Pretense and pretending to be someone that you are not only works in the short term, if at all. You're working to develop a lifelong brand. You are developing a personal brand or a brand for your company that will stand the test of time and pay off with an increasing, continual, residual cash flow.

KEY POINT: You should start seeing a distinctive brand for you, a road map; a picture of you in words that looks entirely different from anyone you know.

You possess a unique set of values, skills, and talents that are marketable and differentiate you from the thousands of others seeking the same role or pursuing similar futures.

We often hide who we are and what we stand for, afraid that it will keep us from the jobs that we desire. If you can be who you were 'born to be' and stand for your beliefs, doors of opportunity will be opened to you. You will be provided with success and distinction that will move you into the right roles that will provide you options to work for the company that best fits you.

What is Your Maximum Potential?

We often do an excellent job as adults of evaluating potential in our children, our nieces or nephews, our mentees, and our employees. Sometimes, however, we don't do as adequate a job of assessing our own potential. What are you capable of achieving? To what heights could you attain? What desires to achieve have you left behind in your childhood or early adult years that need to be revived and resuscitated?

You probably have much more potential than you've ever considered. You have probably set your goals too low and conveniently left your dreams and aspirations behind you. Closely evaluate your potential. Look at your skills and talents and experiences as if you were looking at those of a stranger. Project 'stretch positions' and consider paths that could catapult you closer to the position that best utilizes your skills and talents. Dream a dream. Yes, you read that correctly. Create a dream that incorporates the life that you want to live and the desires of your heart. Write it down. Create 'first steps.' What actions would you start with to move you closer to your dream at heart?

What are you worth? It's possible, even easily foreseeable, that given the right company and the right position for you, you could be worth two or three times what you are currently making. We often undervalue ourselves. We cut ourselves short, and in doing so, we live less than amazing lives doing jobs that are less than exciting or fulfilling. We settle. We get trapped in mediocrity and we stop seeking 'the WOW factor.' I'm asking you to dream up the YOU Brand and to dream up your WOW. I want you to calculate the maximum potential that you believe that you can earn. Then ask two or three of your biggest fans, "What do you believe that I am capable of achieving? What do you believe my maximum earning potential is?" You may be surprised, probably shocked, at the answers. My first response from one of the executives that knows me well and I greatly respect was that I was worth a million dollars a year (no, it didn't come with a job offer). That was more than I'd set as my own potential. I had undervalued the possibilities. Have you undervalued your possibilities? Are you looking at your potential with an open perspective?

If you are jobless, have you considered a stair step path to where you want to arrive? A job, any job, in a company that you admire is better than no job at all. Start somewhere. It is a bit like a battle with weight. Losing weight is better in small quantities than not at all.

Get your foot in the door. Start by accepting that 'first' role. Figure your maximum potential and then move upward and onward toward your earning potential and position that you desire. Ask someone that interviews you to place you in a lower level position that will put your skills to work, assuming they cannot hire you for the position that you applied for because it is 'frozen.' Use your ingenuity. Strategize and plan a way to 'start' somewhere. Companies often promote from within. Get within. Get in the door. Move it!

❖   ❖   ❖

KEY POINT: We get trapped in mediocrity and we stop seeking 'the WOW factor.' Have you stopped looking for WOW in your work life?

❖   ❖   ❖

Personal Brand "To Do" List

Chapter 4: The Cornerstones of your brand
- o What values do you stand for?
- o Incorporate these into your brand
- o Be sure that you are true to yourself
- o Think about your maximum potential

CHAPTER 11
Hall of Famers

CHAPTER 10
Being Unique

CHAPTER 9
Hootsuite & Tweetdeck

CHAPTER 8
Facebook & Twitter

CHAPTER 7
LinkedIn & Plaxo

CHAPTER 6
The Google Effect

CHAPTER 5
Advertising Your Brand

CHAPTER 4
The Cornerstones Of Your Brand

CHAPTER 3
Creating Your Brand

CHAPTER 2
How To Define Your Brand

CHAPTER 1
Why Do You Need This?

Chapter 5: Advertising

You have seen thousands upon thousands of advertisements in your lifetime. Probably more than you've ever wanted to see. These advertisements have created awareness of products and services on the market today. You have formed opinions on these products and services based on the advertisements and, in some cases, personal use of the product or service.

Things you have read and heard others say have played into your perceptions of the brands. How do people talk about you? What do they say about the work you do? Advertisers do not rely simply on 'word of mouth,' they reinforce their message with timely and well-placed advertisements. You can do the same. You can market yourself, your capabilities, and your work in a positive light that brings you opportunities and gets you closer to your maximum potential. You can advertise the YOU brand.

You own the rights to the brand that you are developing. It will be important to carefully consider what, when, and how often you will advertise. Advertisements can take on an assortment of communication modes. We will review several in the next few chapters of the book as we cover the web and social media options for messaging, enforcing, and advertising your brand. Before we cover the often misunderstood and sometimes complex web and social media outlets, let's start simple and basic.

Email

Even an email can 'advertise' and promote your brand if you have positive messages that reinforce your brand values and document results that you have achieved at work. You and your team can do amazing things, but if no one knows, than you're doing nothing to promote yourself and ensure that you're building a value-based brand. You make it simple for others to take credit if you do not. You will not be the one promoted and receiving additional pay and benefits if you are not recognized for your contributions.

Begin to practice regular communication of accomplishments in your area. Think of it as your obligation to keep everyone in your circle of influence informed on current operations with and around you. Announcements, updates, and other pertinent notifications should go out to notify others of information that might affect them. Executives who have climbed the corporate ladder have become experts at this.

Did your team just accomplish a significant task? First, determine the audience for such a message. We often forget this step in a successful career. Think of it this way. It does no good to be GREAT if no one knows that you are great. It is a necessary component of your career path and promotion plans to make sure that YOU and your team are recognized. That list should include everyone you work with on your team, your leader, and the entire leadership team of the company. You are building a brand.

This announcement/update should be brief, contain bulleted lists, and recognize all that contributed to the accomplishment. A template is provided next.

Bethany **W**illiams

To: Leadership Team, Deployment Team, Marketing Team, Engineering Team (etc.)

From: You

_____ made significant
(company name)

strides forward today when _____
                                                    (team name)
completed the project to _____ .
                                          (x, y or z)

The goals of this initiative include:
* Improving customer xyz
* Improving employee satisfaction
* Lowering cost to provide services
   (insert goals here)

This couldn't have been accomplished without the dedication and commitment of our team. Many thanks to _____,_____,_____ .
(list the participants)

Again, many thanks for a job well done.

Please feel free to contact me with any questions.
(Name) (Title) (Phone number) (Email address)

##

In building a brand, the more often you see/hear or notice the brand, the more successful the brand is. As we apply this to YOU, as a brand, it is important that YOU and your successes be 'seen' often. Anywhere from six to ten of the 'successful completion of significant' projects emails or goal attainments should go out directly from you annually. I know that part of you is thinking, "Do I really want to go through all of this?" Well, how badly do you want to succeed? What if I told you that following this plan would lead you to a higher salary, absolutely. Companies PAY MORE for a 'brand' from which they know what to expect. As you build yourself up to be a performer, with abilities to get things done (and they will know since you will be telling them), you will be recognized, promoted, increase your earnings, and achieve your dream position or job. You will ensure that you are not laid off or fired because they didn't know what you'd accomplished. Better yet, someone else will not be promoted for the work you do. (Yes, this happens all the time.)

Advertisers sit around thinking of different ways to attract your attention as a consumer. They mail you different kinds of envelopes, and use all sorts of tactics to be noticed. Creativity can lend a hand in your pursuit of enhancing your brand. Email has become somewhat passé. It is losing its effectiveness. You can, on occasion, print memos and deliver them to the desktop or chair of senior leadership. They will stand out because they are different from other communications. Or consider delivering a memo made completely of chocolate. That'll get noticed.

Expanding Your Target Market

Often you are publicizing your wins and accomplishments to only a small, core group of people in your department or work group area. In order to develop and build a strong brand, think of others outside this group to include in your brand public relations and advertising recipients. Maybe you will decide to summarize your accomplishments twice a year for your entire leadership team. Consider a once a year touch point with the CEO. He/she doesn't know who you are? Well, that is an even better reason to consider it. If you are in senior leadership and you communicate regularly with the leadership team, you should consider communicating your accomplishments to executives in other companies in your industry. Think long and hard to create a list of people that will be your target market.

It may be everyone in your network (whether this is an old-fashioned Rolodex, your Outlook address book, or some of the social media lists that we will address in later chapters).

If your target market isn't identified, it will be hard to create an advertising plan. Begin building your target market list. Add people to the list that would need to know of your success because of the aspirations that you may have to work at that company, in that department, in that role, or you simply need to build awareness to sell your consulting skills, services or your company.

This is another good example of where we often think too small. A variety of people should be on your list. If you are considering a different role or position in early retirement, or as your next career step, key people from that company and departmental area should be on your target list.

Widen, broaden, and deepen this list to include all potential *opportunities*, with your ultimate goal of achieving maximum exposure.

Brand YOU

Remember the Message

Communication often gets lost because we communicate with too many words, and inconsistent messaging. In Chapter 3, you created brand messages for the YOU brand. You decided what values you stand for and how you want to be known. These are now the keys to your advertising and messaging.

Those brand statements about you are what you are publicizing and disseminating to your target audience. Everything you do won't exactly line up to your brand goals and messaging. You will only publicize and advertise messages that further promote your positioning and brand that you want delivered. Advertisers sometimes go astray when they try to promote too many messages. Stick to your core message. Promote those two or three things that you want to be known for. Consistently communicate actions and activities that support those brand messages and reinforce your skill sets and capabilities in your core areas.

Make it Stick! Stand Out from the Crowd

Consider hiring a writer to take your ideas and form them into a well-written message. Develop a slogan. Make a logo. Create a well-developed word and graphic picture that depicts you and who you are as an employee. Be distinct and unusual. Be yourself.

You are not your job title. You are not a business manager, architect or accountant. You are a compilation of the characteristics and skill sets that you use in your position. You are the skills and talents that, if packaged properly, will pay off for you in increased business opportunities and a better future for yourself.

Think slick. Think of well-polished ideas. Think of how you would describe yourself in the best light possible. Think of yourself as a new product that Sony or Apple has just developed. How would you describe and package the product to be appealing and purchasable? What would make you want to buy it? Why would a company pay for your services? What do you have to offer?

KEY POINT: Develop a slogan. Make a logo. Create a well-developed word and graphic picture that depicts you and who you are as an employee.

In order to think slick, you will need to research some of your competition. Think of people in your industry whom you consider to have similar skills and experience to yours. Research them. Look up their bios. Explore their experience and employment history on LinkedIn (www.LinkedIn.com).

Put on the proverbial 'thinking cap' of an owner, CEO or hiring manager. What would motivate them to hire you as opposed to him/her? This is a new economy. Critical thinking is necessary. Critical personal brand development is a requirement. You will not be able to continue to grow and thrive unless you retool and rethink. It is time to get cracking. Brand development is a necessity of the new economy and a well-developed brand can and will pay off handsomely.

KEY POINT: This is a new economy. Critical thinking is necessary. Critical personal brand development is a requirement. You will not be able to continue to grow and thrive unless you retool and rethink.

Personal Brand "To Do" List

Chapter 5: Advertising Your Brand

o Determine how you will advertise your brand

o Make a plan to promote yourself through email

o Create a list of "targets": people to whom you'd like to communicate your brand message

Brand YOU

CHAPTER 11
Hall of Famers

CHAPTER 10
Being Unique

CHAPTER 9
Hootsuite & Tweetdeck

CHAPTER 8
Facebook & Twitter

CHAPTER 7
LinkedIn & Plaxo

CHAPTER 6
The Google Effect

CHAPTER 5
Advertising Your Brand

CHAPTER 4
The Cornerstones Of Your Brand

CHAPTER 3
Creating Your Brand

CHAPTER 2
How To Define Your Brand

CHAPTER 1
Why Do You Need This?

Chapter 6: The Google Effect

Since when did "Google" become a verb? It seems that it has. How many times a day do you hear someone say "Google it"? Google has become a modern day brand giant! Google yourself. What comes up? Are you easy to find? Do other people with the same name come up? Based on your search criteria and the amount of names and data that come up, you can decide whether you want to brand yourself with a middle initial or a nickname.

Your goal is for it to be easy for people to find you. If someone had a fantastic job offer for you, wouldn't you want him to be able to find you?

Make yourself findable. The next few chapters will walk you through free internet options to raise awareness of who you are and allow you to brand and market your capabilities. We will also cover paid options to increase awareness of you or your company.

Through this amplified exposure plan, you will increase others' ability to find you when they reach out to find you.

Claiming Sources and Content

There are several sources on the internet that aggregate and collate information about you. Sometimes aggregated data has correct links, but often it has collected sources that should not be linked to you. Once logging into these resources (example Spoke, www.spoke.com), you are able to claim the correct sources of information and detach incorrect sources. You want to be in a position to control the information that is linked to you. It does you no good to have inaccurate data attached to you that could be affecting your brand in a negative way.

For those of you that feel that you don't have the time for this research, consider hiring a college student or a public relations firm to aid you in your research and follow up. The new economy and increased competition require it. Some companies have their marketing teams input the data for their senior-level leadership teams.

For businesses, you also should claim information. If there is a listing for your business location, you should claim the location in Google Places at www.google.com/places. Type in key location information about your business and confirm information. Add specific details that make your business more appealing to your customers. Consider adding your hours of operation and a picture that represents what your business looks like.

If you are opening a new business in a physical location, go to Google Places and enter the location. Enter the specific details that make it sound fabulous. You will receive a postcard in 2-3 weeks at the physical location for you to confirm the address and information prior to the listing showing up.

Your Own Domain

There are several ways to own your brand and sell yourself, but one that I've seen to provide proven success over and over again is purchasing an internet location that you can brand specifically for YOU. You can determine the look and feel of the website, as well as determining the name of the site. The proliferation of the web has made owning your own web site quite economical. You can buy a website that is role specific, for example CaliforniaAccountingGuy.com (for eleven US dollars a year) or LondonCPA.com (for only a few Euros a year), or one that is specific to your name; for example, www.BethanyannWilliams.org.

You don't have to possess technical skills to buy a domain. Some of the domains available for purchase are only 85 cents a year. You can buy a three-year web location for as little as two or three US dollars or Euros.

Step One:
Buy the domain and figure out the name you'd like to be listed as. There are several options for each country, listed here is information for the US and the UK: 1and1.co.uk, GoDaddy.com, MyDomains.com, and NamesDirect.com, are just a few of your numerous options.

Any one of these will work perfectly fine. Each service gives you an opportunity to discover naming options that are available. It is possible that the name that you'd like to buy may not be currently available.

Step Two:
Next, either create a web site or hire someone to create one for you. This step doesn't need to happen the instant you purchase your new web address. However, when you are ready, domains come with easy tools that you can use to create your own site, or hire someone to do it for you.

Gone are the days that you must understand coding languages and detailed technical knowledge to use the tools provided. You might consider giving it a swing. You may find that it is not as hard as you had thought it would be.

If you'd rather hire someone to create one for you, there are numerous options from teenagers that create them at home to reputable companies that can create sites for you. You have the option for US- or UK-based resources, or even hiring resources overseas. I have often used www.GetFriday.com resources to develop my web sites. They provide a cost-efficient way to create a well-constructed layout for a very reasonable price. You determine how much you want to spend to begin building your brand.

The finished product should reflect YOU. It should be about you, your capabilities, your aspirations, and specifics about what makes you unique. It should reflect the brand that you are developing. It should incorporate the messages that you have created in a previous chapter of this book. You can always revamp and update the site as you progress in your career and successes. The beginning one that you develop should be just that, a launching pad for your trajectory.

Google Alerts

Well-developed strategies can include the development of Google alerts. Google can alert you when you or your company is written about online. These alerts scour the internet, on vigilant alert for times that you are showing up online. They are easy to set up and you can receive a weekly email summarizing any place where you have appeared in online media. Small businesses use this as a way to ensure that they know what is being said about their company.

A Google "How to":

Step 1: Login to your gmail account, or create one if you don't have one at www.gmail.com. Having this free account will allow you to set up the rules and alerts for notification.

Step 2: Once you have created your gmail account and have logged in, across the top of the page is a listing of available functionality. Click on 'More,' and then 'Even More,' and a new page will open. Locate the section titled 'Alerts' under Specialized Search.

Step 3: This simple tool will allow you to search for terms, by entering the following information:

Search Terms: Fill the pertinent information into the form.

What are you looking for? List your name or the company name about which you'd like to receive alerts.

You can preview results. If you'd like to see what will come up with the alert that you've set up, click on preview results.

Type:	Everything ▼
How often:	Once a week ▼
Volume:	Only the best results ▼
Deliver to:	bethanyawilliams@gmail.com ▼

It will auto fill in your gmail account for alert delivery. You can setup your gmail account to forward on to an email that you use regularly.

Step 4: Voila! You have created your rule. The rules engine will 'catch' the information that you've requested that it scan the web for and you will begin getting your alerts within seven days.

Companies are beginning to watch these alerts and many have included it in their brand strategies. It wouldn't' hurt to incorporate this into your brand strategy as you more fully develop it and your plan matures.

Personal Brand "To Do" List

Chapter 6: The Google Effect

- o Google yourself
- o Make yourself 'findable'
- o Claim internet sources for yourself, i.e. www.spokeo.com
- o Set up Google alerts

Brand YOU

CHAPTER 11
Hall of Famers

CHAPTER 10
Being Unique

CHAPTER 9
Hootsuite & Tweetdeck

CHAPTER 8
Facebook & Twitter

CHAPTER 7
LinkedIn & Plaxo

CHAPTER 6
The Google Effect

CHAPTER 5
Advertising Your Brand

CHAPTER 4
The Cornerstones Of Your Brand

CHAPTER 3
Creating Your Brand

CHAPTER 2
How To Define Your Brand

CHAPTER 1
Why Do You Need This?

Chapter 7: LinkedIn and Plaxo

LinkedIn

LinkedIn (www.LinkedIn.com) is a business-networking site. It provides a great way to create a personal brand that represents your work life. Do not confuse this with Facebook or believe that this is just a way to chat with connections. Many jobs are found and resources are being identified daily on LinkedIn. It provides the ability for the recruiters to contact employees that may not be looking for work as well as to search for employees that are looking for work but don't know about opportunities that exist or where to apply.

Now that you've gotten to the point of acceptance of the importance of your brand and decided that you will enforce your brand with your online presence, now you can either develop your LinkedIn profile at www.LinkedIn.com or refine your profile to attract the attention of the viewers that search for and view your profile.

Ever read an ad that made you want to run to the store and make a purchase? Your goal is to create an online billboard that appeals to the potential customers, employers, future equity partners, employees that you may someday hire, or employers that may hire you.

You will aim to create an appealing representation of the work that you have done and continue to do. You will highlight your interests and passions, and the reason that someone may want to seek you out to offer you a better position, equity for your company, or hire the services of you or your company. Your online billboard should make them want to bookmark your page for future reference.

So, how do you get started? Follow these three easy steps.

Step 1: Create a Profile:
If you don't have a profile, log into www.LinkedIn.com and create a free profile. This is your opportunity to advertise your capabilities and begin to build your personal brand. Many of you have five different resumes that you are using depending on what you apply for. LinkedIn is a summary of who you are and where you've been, and where you are going. It is a singular representation of you. You will combine all of the varying resumes that you have together into one brand and one profile.

For the unemployed:
Your LinkedIn profile should represent what the BEST job for you would be. What are you passionate about? What are you skilled and created to do? If you got the job you wanted, what would it be?

For the employed:
If you are employed, this profile represents your 'Brand.' What do you want to be known for at work? What promotion would you like to have? Position your write-up for the next step in your career OR if you are external facing (executive/sales, etc.) create a profile that advertises the message you would want distributed externally. Use this as a billboard. It is your own personal Brand Billboard™.

Step 2: Build a Network:
Next you will begin to add contacts to your network. If

you were out of work, who would be the first five people you would call? Start with these five. Slowly, as you meet people, add them to your network. This will begin to show value when you need an introduction to a potential employer, investor, or business partner. This is today, but will provide insurance for tomorrow and a better way to work today when you need to interact with other organizations.

Step 3: Find a Resource:

Do you need to hire someone? Do you need to find someone that you used to work with, but don't know where they are working now? Do you want to buy something from a company, but don't know whom to call? You can find all this and much more on LinkedIn with a quick and easy search. You are on your way to a great start. If you have created a profile, link to mine at http://www.linkedin.com/in/bethanywilliams. I want to hear from you.

The results have been dramatic. Out-of-work executives have secured interviews immediately after updating or starting a LinkedIn profile. Recruiters, paid to fill positions, are actively searching for candidates. They search the LinkedIn database regularly and often for key words that would be reflected in people that may fit the bill for a company with an open position. If you show up in a search, and your profile is well written, they will reach out to you to measure your interest level.

LinkedIn options allow you to state whether or not you want to be contacted for these interactions. You can create a profile, yet set your privacy settings to keep recruiters and employers from contacting you. You control the access that others have to you.

Read on for more pieces of advice on creating, editing, and revising your LinkedIn profile.

Step Away from the Title
Within the corporate world, we have become addicted to titles. These titles within our company DO NOT mean anything to people outside of our company. You need to explain what you do in an industry standard way that would appeal to people at ANY company, not just your company.

Recognize the Internal Benefits
If you are working in a big company, there are internal benefits to beefing up your LinkedIn profile. There could be important leaders within your company that do not KNOW YOU and do not KNOW WHAT YOU DO. This is not good positioning. If a position comes open that you would be great for, they WILL NOT think of you if they do not KNOW YOU.

Write a Fantastic Advertisement
Your LinkedIn profile is really much more than an online resume. It is an advertisement for you. It should show the return on investment that companies have benefited from having YOU on their staff. It should be a results-oriented view of YOU. The reader should be excited about what YOU could do for HIS/HER COMPANY.

Surf Through LinkedIn Profiles
What JUMPS out at you? What amazes you? Your profile should AMAZE others. It is a competitive landscape.

SPEND SOME TIME ON IT. Refine it until it jumps off the page. Find profiles that you like.

I recently helped an executive re-do his profile and he secured three interviews the next week. Recruiters are watching. They are looking for candidates. They may be looking for you, but you may have done such a poor job of selling yourself that they can't find you. Make it easier for them to find you. Accept the online branding capabilities and excel at creating an exciting and off-the-charts profile.

I regularly meet unemployed job seekers. My first piece of advice is always the same: Create a LinkedIn profile. Recruiters will look there for potential candidates and you have a much better chance of being found. Take some of the effort and shift it to the recruiters instead of doing all the work yourself. Use the tools available to you to jump yourself into the present. Use this amazing tool to catapult your brand and your opportunities.

Keep enhancing your profile. It will pay off.

KEY POINT: Your goal is to create an online billboard that appeals to the potential customers, employers, future equity partners, employees that you may someday hire, or employers that may hire you.

Plaxo Social Networking Tool

Let's discuss Plaxo (www.Plaxo.com). This tool allows you to sync your contacts from email, phones and you're your social networks into one location, making them portable and usable from any device.   You can opt in for access to their personal assistant that will enable you to receive updates and duplicate checking in your database of contacts. This is a helpful tool for sales executives and others that have very large networks to manage.

Visualize Plaxo as a smart address book, keeping your contacts in sync and information readily available, accurate, and easily accessible from any of your devices.

With over 50 million address book accounts, there are certainly a good share of consumers that use this tool to manage their contacts. Your contacts, in many careers, are your lifeblood. With a tool like Plaxo, you ensure that regardless of your current employment, you have access to important connections that you have made throughout your career.

Birthday Notices

One of my favorite features is the birthday notices. Plaxo emails upcoming birthdays and gives you an easy opportunity to send electronic cards with integrated functionality that makes it simplistic. It allows you to 'keep up' with birthdays you wouldn't normally have on your radar and completes the email address and date in the electronic cards functionality making it simple to use. It will widen your ability to be thoughtful with people in your span of influence.

Plaxo 'How To':
It is simple to get started.

1) Log on to www.plaxo.com

2) Start a simple profile

3) Connect to a few people that you know. I expect an invitation:

www.plaxo.com/directory/profile/51539819800 /.../Bethany/Williams

4) Watch, post and learn.

Be sure to enjoy the journey.

Personal Brand "To Do" List

Chapter 7: LinkedIn & Plaxo
o Create a LinkedIn profile at
   www.linkedin.com
o Check out Plaxo www.plaxo.com
o Continue to enhance your LinkedIn profile,
   finding examples that you like

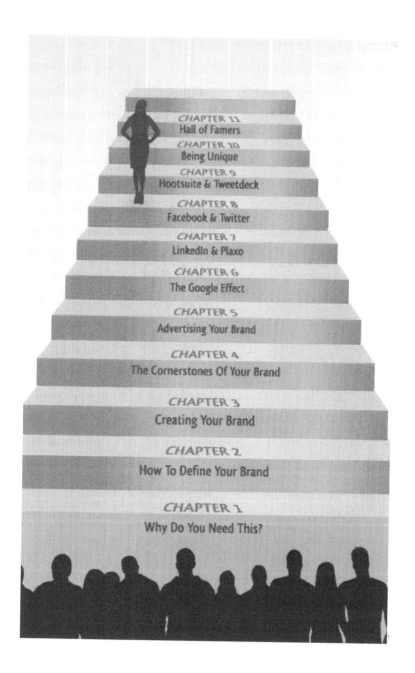

Chapter 8: Using Facebook & Twitter

Facebook
Facebook (www.Facebook.com) is a social networking site that allows you to connect with friends, family and co-workers in a 'water cooler,' backyard BBQ kind of way. It is used by many as a personal network, allowing people to connect to people with whom they have developed personal relationships.

This is networking and relationship management for the 21st century. You say you have no time to connect with your family, friends and co-workers. A-ha! Facebook is born. It provides the ability for you to work yourself to death and still have somewhat of a social life, at least pretend to digitally.

Easily post a picture and Bam! You have just shared that picture with ALL your friends, family and co-workers in your network. Maybe you would like to go to dinner and you would like to see who can go? Post a comment and get an instant answer from one of your friends. Need to hire someone for an opening in your department? Post a request and Voila! Instant information is at your fingertips.

If you are thinking that you don't have time for Facebook, then you don't see the timesaving benefit of it. It could save you from writing 10 emails. It could prevent you from making five phone calls for information that you seek. It is like Google that searches ONLY your network.

Businesses are using Facebook for zero dollar advertising. They are building a community of followings, advertising specials and new deals, driving traffic to their web site and messaging news and content regularly to build their brand and increase sales.

Step 1: Create a Personal Facebook Account

If you don't have your own account, log into www.Facebook.com and create a free Facebook account. This is your opportunity to find schoolmates that you wish you knew where they are and what they are doing, or that friend from 15 years ago that you have never called. Want to find an old college buddy or connect to an old flame? Facebook might be the perfect place to start.

For the unemployed:

Your Facebook account can help you connect to an old friend that can get you an interview at his/her place of work. This is relationship networking at its best. If you are out of work, YOU MUST start a Facebook account. It is one way to 'network' your way into a job opening. Start an account. Post comments about the type of job that you are looking for. Ask your network to introduce you into open positions in their companies. Do not resist asking.

Step 2: Find your Family/Friends/Co-workers:

Next, you will begin to add friends to your network. You have that list in your head of people that you've been wondering about. Search for them. Try to locate them. If you connect to one person that you know, look to see with whom they are connected. You may see friends of yours in common with the friends you have on your list. It is easy to find friends and connect.

Step 3: Post some pictures and a comment or two:

Find some family pictures that you adore and load them into your profile. Fill in a comment that you feel led to write. You are on your way to a great start. Log in whenever you have the time. It will wait for you. You don't have to worry about it feeling neglected.

Creating a Facebook Page for Your Company or Small Business

Many have found the benefits of advertising, increased awareness, and ability to build community through creation of a Facebook page for your company. Facebook functionality allows the 'company' to have the page and erases older worries that the person maintaining it quits and you lose the connection to the page. Log into your personal Facebook account. Find an entry for 'Create a Page' functionality.

Select the descriptor that best fits the page you'd like to create. Are you advertising a business, company, place or product? Are you a performing artist, or advertising an entertainment venue? Select on the best fit.

Load an image that represents your logo or a picture representation of your company. Promote the page and invite others to explore it. Post news events and special offers there for others to see.

Brand YOU

Twitter

We can't do an overview of creating your brand using social networking without browsing the benefits of Twitter. It is ever evolving. It is a bit like the evolution of internet use. It consistently changed, almost faster than individuals and business could keep up. That is how social networking advances.

As participants use it and gain benefits, they document those benefits. The functionality increases, tools are built around the peripherals, and Voila! You have something that barely resembles what it began as. That is Twitter.

Today Twitter is, I believe, a great way to get a message out. It allows you to track industries and key companies or people that represent your interests. You don't have to have a smart phone to use Twitter. Any internet-connected computer can access Twitter.

Bethany Williams

Twitter is not for the faint at heart, or shouldn't be your first attempt into social networking. This is solely my opinion. I suggest opening an account, and tracking a few industries, key CEOs or persons of interest.

I have gained great work-related knowledge from using Twitter the short period of time that I have used it. I track the CandidCIO and have learned great insight from his tweets. I follow healthcare technology expert Harry Greenspun and enjoy following the Zappos CEO and a few other industry markers that I find of interest. I have a personal Twitter (WinLifeStrategy) that represents my passion to encourage executives to excel as well as a work Twitter (BethanyZirMed) that enables me to represent ZirMed and our product offerings and aids that we have for the healthcare market.

Step 1: Go to www.Twitter.com
Open an account.

Step 2: Load a picture and fill out a basic profile. This will be the easiest of profiles since it allows a very minimal number of characters.

Step 3: Begin to follow persons of interest, political personalities, key executives or industries of interest to you.

Step 4: Check in occasionally to read any direct messages to you and occasionally 'tweet' away.

Brand **YOU**

Personal Brand "To Do" List

Chapter 8: Facebook & Twitter
- Create a Facebook account at www.facebook.com
- Check out Twitter at www.twitter.com

Brand YOU

CHAPTER 11
Hall of Famers

CHAPTER 10
Being Unique

CHAPTER 9
Hootsuite & Tweetdeck

CHAPTER 8
Facebook & Twitter

CHAPTER 7
LinkedIn & Plaxo

CHAPTER 6
The Google Effect

CHAPTER 5
Advertising Your Brand

CHAPTER 4
The Cornerstones Of Your Brand

CHAPTER 3
Creating Your Brand

CHAPTER 2
How To Define Your Brand

CHAPTER 1
Why Do You Need This?

Chapter 9: New Generation Social Networking Tools

HootSuite

The next phase of social networking education takes you to HootSuite (www.hootsuite.com). HootSuite takes you to the next level of Twitter. You will love it. I like the ability to categorize and sift through tidbits of information.

For me, HootSuite is like reading my OWN personal newspaper with the addition of messages that are there JUST for me. Imagine reading the *New York Times* with a column that says, "You are a Great Mom! I'm glad you took the kids to the park." Now that is a reading activity that I can enjoy (laugh).

If you have begun using Twitter, Facebook or the many other sites, it may be time for you to at least explore HootSuite. As I learn more, I'll update you on my website at www.BethanyWilliams.org.

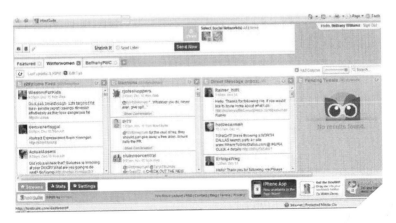

Brand **YOU**

TweetDeck

TweetDeck advertises itself as 'your personal real-time browser, connecting you with your contacts across Twitter, Facebook, MySpace, LinkedIn, Foursquare, Google Buzz and more.' TweetDeck is now part of Twitter.

TweetDeck and many of the new tools combine social media feeds and allow you to choose ONE place to get all the information across a variety of social media tools. You could organize all your messages into one space, organize and update your Facebook page, and see a single view of information easily displayed for you to see, view, use, and converse.

Xobni.com

What if you could combine all of the social media streams on a person, collate the information, and make it readily available with email information to give you a whole view of anyone that you are emailing or corresponding with? That describes Xobni.com. Xobni.com describes itself as the ability to take all the emails you've exchanged (Gmail, Yahoo!, Outlook), SMS messages, and phone calls, finds all the people that you've communicated with, and automatically creates a complete social profile for each of them, making it available to you on any device. They have been featured in an assortment of well-known periodicals and online popular destinations and downloaded by more than seven million people.

These social media tools are developing faster than we—the public—can absorb them. Xobni.com can integrate to your Outlook and allow you to see pertinent information as you go about your daily business of work or play. It inserts information at your fingertips just when you need it, allows you to view it if you like, when you like, as you have need for the information. It is simply brilliant.

I believe more and more of these tools will arrive on the market to make social media easier and more fluid. It will flow better into the activities that you naturally do. The market is demanding ease of use and pertinent information in the nick of time. The demand will push companies to innovate and those innovations will press the limits of what we have seen to date.

The tools listed in this book have progressed in listing from the simplest to the more sophisticated. You can select those that work for your particular industry and position. Various needs will require varying tools, the way positions require different skill sets.

I like that Xobni.com allows information at fingertip access without requiring me to go search for it. It brings me the needed information.

Find them on the web at http://xobni.com. Try loading the tool on your Blackberry or iPhone.

Spokeo

As tools evolution continues, consider looking at Spokeo, the next generation of online white pages directories. Per their website, Spokeo is a people search engine that organizes vast quantities of white pages listings, social information, and other people-related data from a large variety of public sources. Spokeo describes itself as 'not your grandmother's white pages'. I would agree.

They charge for some of their services, allowing query capabilities for basic information, but charge for deeper and more in depth information. They pull from public records, and have detailed information on housing size, number of bedrooms, neighborhood wealth listings, and information on residents in the home and education levels. It is detailed and allows for easy access to a variety of information that once took a considerable amount of time to research. Find them on the web at www.spokeo.com.

Talent.Me

Talent.me is career networking on facebook. It is about using the power of social media to find jobs and opportunities. User's log in via their Facebook. Their message; gt endorsed, get referrals, get jobs. A recruiter from PWC sent me a link to join this site. Their advice is to use your social network to grow professionally.

Many of the new tools build upon each other. You are usually not required as a user to re-do profiles again and again. The new tools are built with the ability to log onto your other profiles and copy data and information over.

Keep a list of places that you have information so that when you do make a job change, you can correct all data sources. Online content management for your brand will be a component that you will have to manage and maintain once you have developed an online presence. The good part is that data will change infrequently, and data changes won't be required usually more often than annually or every other year.

Once your profile is built, there are jobs that you can view and apply for. It is similar to other capabilities that we have covered in previous chapters.

Talent.me is Facebook's attempt to re-create a LinkedIn type piece of functionality that exposes you to job opportunities. We have yet to see whether or not it will catch on as fast and fluidly as LinkedIn has. LinkedIn has been amazing at building functionality that works and creating user friendly interfaces for us to view and consume the information.

Branch Out

Facebook has also developed 'Branch Out'. They are working diligently to expand their offerings and this is touted as a career service. Once familiar with one of the career development tools, it is difficult to move from tool to tool easily. Each has slightly varying functionality and capabilities.

Explore available options and find the tools that fit you best. Stick to a core and don't try to be on all the sites.

In preparation for the research for this book, I isgned up for every imaginable site and found myself in a social media craze, confused at the multitude of sites available and the varying features and functions developed for the users.

I still have found LinkedIn to be my favorite tool, but you have to choose the tools that work for you.

Below is a compilation of Social Networking options discussed in Chapters 6-9.

Brand YOU

Social Networking Summary Table	Description
Facebook http://www.facebook.com/	**Facebook** helps you connect and share with the people in your life.
Plaxo http://www.plaxo.com/	**Plaxo.com** is the world's leading online address book, hosting over 50 million address book accounts.
LinkedIn http://www.linkedin.com/	Over 120 million professionals use **LinkedIn** to exchange information, ideas and opportunities. Control your professional identity online, stay informed about your contacts and industry, and find the people and knowledge you need to achieve your goals.
HootSuite https://hootsuite.com/	**HootSuite** allows you to have multiple contributors to your social profiles without sharing passwords. Assign messages for follow-up and track responses. From help desk to marketing, engage audiences at every level of your organization.
TweetDeck http://www.tweetdeck.com/	**TweetDeck** is your personal real-time browser, connecting you across Twitter, Facebook, MySpace, LinkedIn, Foursquare, Google Buzz, etc.

[continued on next page]

Social Networking Summary Table	Description
Twitter http://twitter.com/	**Twitter** is a real-time information network that connects you to the latest information about what you find interesting. Simply find the public streams you find most compelling and follow the conversations.
Xobni https://www.xobni.com/	**Xobni** offers a unique and intelligent way to view and search your contacts and email through Outlook so you can spend less time searching for important information in your inbox & the web.
Spokeo http://www.spokeo.com/	**Spokeo** is a new-age white pages, aggregating data from many online and offline sources (such as phone directories, social networks, photo albums, marketing surveys, mailing lists, government censuses, real estate listings).
Talent.me https://talent.me/	**Talent.me** is a professional networking app on Facebook. Talent.me works to help you leverage your friend network and make it work for your career advancement.
BranchOut http://apps.facebook.com/branchout/about/home	**BranchOut** is the largest professional network on Facebook.

Brand YOU

Why Network? And Why Brand?

I still hear many of you saying, "Why should I spend time Networking?" "When will I find the time to build a personal brand?" You get busy, and you don't network or take the steps to build a brand. You think of hundreds of other things to do. I still think one thing rings true. You will never be disappointed by spending time networking or building your brand. Well thought out connections that you've made in your networks and steller personal brands that you have developed will pay off. Together, they help people find jobs, resolve issues, and move up the career ladder, and achieve positions and projects that they love to do. It is a MUST to both network and brand.

You should network regularly. You should consistently work to keep up your network by emailing/calling or writing people in your network just to say 'hi'. If you were to lose your job today, who would be the first five people that you'd call to help you find another job? Those five people should be on your networking 'to call' list. Don't wait until something happens at your job for you to reach out to your stay in touch. I am not asking you to 'connect' with tons of people, I'm asking you to connect authentically to 4 or 5 people annually that you geniunly like and have something in common with that you would call if you were out of work. I am constantly bombarded with people who have lost their jobs and are now reaching out to me. I may not have spoken to them in five, ten, or fifteen years. I do not know what they've been up to, how their career has progressed, or where they have been working. I am unable to recommend companies and positions for them without key pieces of information that will take considerable time to obtain. Don't put your network contacts in this position. Help them help you.

Having a network to lean on means that you won't have as hard a time looking for a job. Think about it. It is the toughest job market we've seen in years. What if you didn't have to worry about it because you had built a strong network that ensured jobs within that network. Wouldn't that be worth keeping up with your network?

Think of it like a savings account. If you have made no deposits to the networking account, it is very difficult to make withdrawals. People do not want to ONLY hear from you when you need something. Stay in touch. Network. Help everyone that you can. Pay it forward to make sustainable impacts in other's lives. When you need help, they will be there for you to help you connect and find resources that you need. It will pay off.

◆ ◆ ◆

KEY POINT: One thing rings true: You will never be disappointed by spending time networking or branding. Networks and brands pay off. Together, they help people find jobs, resolve issues and solve problems.

Brand YOU

Personal Brand "To Do" List

Chapter 9: HootSuite & Tweetdeck
- o Evaluate the advantage of HootSuite, www.hootsuite.com, and Tweetdeck , www.tweetdeck.com
- o Plot on your calendar regular intervals to network/touch base with contacts in your network

Brand YOU

CHAPTER 11
Hall of Famers

CHAPTER 10
Being Unique

CHAPTER 9
Hootsuite & Tweetdeck

CHAPTER 8
Facebook & Twitter

CHAPTER 7
LinkedIn & Plaxo

CHAPTER 6
The Google Effect

CHAPTER 5
Advertising Your Brand

CHAPTER 4
The Cornerstones Of Your Brand

CHAPTER 3
Creating Your Brand

CHAPTER 2
How To Define Your Brand

CHAPTER 1
Why Do You Need This?

Chapter 10: Be Unique and Different

You are unique. You have special gifts and talents that differentiate you from others. If you find that you are struggling to stand out from the crowd, these gifts and talents are the key. If you are unsure exactly what your strengths are, there are many paths to discovering exactly what they are. Author Marcus Buckingham talks about discovering your strengths in his books, *Now Discover Your Strengths* and *The Truth About You* (http://vodpod.com/watch/2316307-the-truth-about-you-marcus-buckingham).

When you are able to tap into the strengths that you possess, you will be able to perform at a level where others cannot compete. You will be able to work in a 'zone' above the rest. Learning to tap into your strengths at work will do another thing for you. It will help you to enjoy your work more than you ever have. When you are using the strengths that you have been gifted with, you will be energized and motivated. You will love the components of your job that use your strengths. You will want to volunteer for assignments and projects that are in the areas that you love to do.

Sometimes we shy away from what makes us different from the others around us or we shy away from volunteering to take on projects offered up that we think we would love to do. Fear keeps us from stepping out. It is more important to be unique and celebrate the skills that we have. Take a risk. Make a goal to discover your hidden strengths.

Brand YOU

Discovering core strengths will enable you to move into positions that will utilize your strengths. You will discover jobs that you love and you will stand out from the crowd.

Begin your path to discovery. Find and use your passions and set yourself apart from the crowd. What will be the result? You will find jobs that you love and increase your job security. These are two things that everyone can celebrate.

KEY POINT: Discovering core strengths will enable you to move into positions that will utilize your strengths. You will discover jobs that you love and you will stand out from the crowd.

Personal Brand "To Do" List

Chapter 10: Be Unique

- Re-evaluate: Have you created a brand that is different enough to stand out in a crowded marketplace?
- Celebrate what makes you different
- Find and use your passions

Brand YOU

CHAPTER 11
Hall of Famers

CHAPTER 10
Being Unique

CHAPTER 9
Hootsuite & Tweetdeck

CHAPTER 8
Facebook & Twitter

CHAPTER 7
LinkedIn & Plaxo

CHAPTER 6
The Google Effect

CHAPTER 5
Advertising Your Brand

CHAPTER 4
The Cornerstones Of Your Brand

CHAPTER 3
Creating Your Brand

CHAPTER 2
How To Define Your Brand

CHAPTER 1
Why Do You Need This?

Chapter 11: Amazing Examples of Branding Success

Brand "Hall of Famers"

It wouldn't be invigorating or exciting unless we take a chapter to give you examples of the "hall of famers" in brand management. They have summated to the pinnacles of understanding and used their brands to achieve and succeed. They are noteworthy and provide encouraging examples for your own personal journey.

In this critically competitive market, the brand you develop can catapult your career, the awareness of your services and, ultimately, your worth. Examples throughout this chapter will help you to visualize the brand success that you can attain. Understand thoroughly the summits that you can climb with amazing brands.

Brand YOU

Harry Greenspun, MD

Harry Greenspun, MD

Brand Billboard™: Physician executive focusing on healthcare transformation and technology
Occupation: Senior Advisor
Twitter: harrygreenspun
LinkedIn: http://www.linkedin.com/in/harrygreenspun
Company website: http://www.deloitte.com/global
Wikipedia listing*:
http://en.wikipedia.org/wiki/Harry_Greenspun

I met Harry Greenspun when he was working as a Chief Medical Officer for Northrop Grumman. He was a young, talented physician, articulate, with everything going for him. He didn't have an established brand, and others didn't know him, his talents, or where to find him. We recruited him to Perot Systems Corporation when we needed a Chief Medical Officer. I met with him several times to discuss his goals, his brand, and the heights that he could attain given some attention on his brand. We put a plan in place to develop his brand, market his brand, and catapult his brand to national awareness. It worked!

Within two years, he was named "One of the Healthcare IT Game Changers to Watch" by ExecutiveBiz.com; he co-authored a book with Jim Champy entitled *Re-Engineering Healthcare*; and his brand quickly rose to national attention. Recently I discovered that he even has a Wikipedia listing*. Okay, I'm impressed. With this increased awareness have come new opportunities and offers for new and exciting positions. He has grown his brand to allow himself options. He now gets access to opportunities that he was not afforded prior to establishing his brand. Creating a brand, marketing it, and consistently enforcing it have paid off for Harry.

Brand YOU

Dina Bar-EL of the Dina Bar-EL Fashion Empire

Dina Bar-EL

Brand Billboard™: Fashion Designer to the Stars, bringing elegance and grace to the Red Carpet and applying that brilliance to a global marketplace appealing to fashion savvy women

Occupation: Fashion Designer

Twitter: dinabarel

LinkedIn: http://www.linkedin.com/pub/dina-bar-el/16/4a9/43

Company website: http://www.dinabarel.com/

Several years ago, I met Dina Bar-EL of the Dina Bar-EL Fashion Empire. She is an amazingly brilliant designer that gained significant popularity in 2004 and 2005 when Kate Hudson wore one of her dress designs in the movie "How to Lose a Guy in 10 Days." Since Kate graced the movie set in the stunning yellow satin dress, Dina has been blessed with a brand that is now known worldwide and an ever growing business. You can find her on the web at www.DinaBarEL.com.

Now, she is looking at brand development options that will further expand her business, her market, and the profitability of her business.

Jeb Blount, Author and Sales Expert

Jeb Blount

Brand Billboard™: Published Author and Sales Expert
Occupation: Vice President of Sales
Twitter: jebblount
Blog: http://salesgravy.com/JebsBlog/
LinkedIn: http://www.linkedin.com/in/jebblount
Company website: http://www.kgbdeals.com/national/
Wikipedia listing*:
http://en.wikipedia.org/wiki/Jeb_Bount

Jeb Blount is a sales leader. He has more than 20 years of sales experience. There are thousands of people that match those criteria. Jeb isn't your average sales leader though. He has developed a brand , started a website called Sales Gravy for salesmen and saleswomen everywhere and built an incredible brand that has expanded his reach to a global marketplace. Find him on the web at www.salesgravy.com.

He has taken his brand and brand awareness to a level that allows him to live his passion, which he states is growing people by helping them to find their unique ability and potential. He is able to do this through authoring books, being a seminar leader and a public speaker. He has developed a brand that allows him to live his passion and set him apart from others in the same field in a market wrought with virtually thousands of out of work sales executives. He stands out. He has an amazing brand.

Won-G

Won-G

Brand Billboard™:   Haitian born rapper, Entrepreneur and Philanthropist
Occupation: Musician
Twitter: realsovage
Blog: http://won-g.com/blog/
Bio: http://www.won-g.com/bio.pdf
Company websites: http://www.won-g.com and www.sovagedenim.com and www.onedomeatatime.org
Wikipedia listing*: http://en.wikipedia.org/wiki/Won-G_Bruny

Won-G was raised in Haiti. He self-released his first CD at age 15. Since then, he has released five independent albums and currently lives in Beverly Hills. He enjoys an amazing lifestyle, drives a Rolls Royce Phantom, and is extremely active in the community. He serves as both Haiti's and Unicef's Ambassador of Good Will for children and has a long history of supporting charitable causes such as; Recording Artists, Actors, and Athletes Against Drunk Driving (RADD), Priscilla Presley's Dream Foundation, and Malibu's Bony Pony Ranch, which rehabs underprivileged children and at-risk youth. His videos often include stars like Paris Hilton, Carmen Electra, and Tracey Bingham.

He chooses to reflect a brand broader than solely 'rapper' or musician. He is known for being a rapper, a businessman, a philanthropist, and a role model. He says, "There are so many rebellious kids out there and they need to have opportunities to channel their energy in constructive ways." He wants to use his music and his life to show young people that they can make a difference and make the world a better place.

He started a business venture, Sovage Denim (www.sovagedenim.com), that has created a stylish, high-end denim that boasts the best fit in jeans for all styles.

Not satisfied with solely being a musician, he has built a brand of a musician, an entrepreneur, businessman and a philanthropist. He is a breath of fresh air, very different from most of the stars that you could potentially meet in Beverly Hills.

He understands how his brand plays into his success. He has carefully crafted separate brand messages across his individual brands. He is a man with brand understanding.

Mark Eimer

Mark Eimer

Brand Billboard™: Highly accomplished, results-oriented IT Visionary and Top IT Executive
Occupation: Executive Director of Technology
Twitter: meimer
LinkedIn: http://www.linkedin.com/in/
Company website: http://www.ukhealthcare.uky.edu/

When I originally heard Mark Eimer's name, he was working for Perot Systems Corporation and working on the Stanford Healthcare account in California. They were implementing a new electronic health record and changes were fast and furious, the environment tough and demanding. He developed a reputation that embodied one word: Results. He developed a reputation for getting things done. When people thought of Mark's IT role, they thought of 'no nonsense, cut the crap, and get it done.' Remember the outside-in views of your work that you did in Chapter 1? These are the things that Mark hears when he does this Q&A with those that know him.

He then worked to create a LinkedIn profile that built upon his strengths. He worked to raise visibility and increase his job opportunities. He wanted options. He wanted the ability to pick a great position that fit him. He often hears, "We heard about you; we heard that you can get things done." The message resonates across healthcare facilities that desperately need to be able to get the job done with regard to their information technology.

As a hiring manager, Mark often asks the people that he interviews to give him one adjective that they would use to describe themself. That one adjective then helps him assess their 'brand' and determine who to hire.

Mark understands brand. He has developed a great brand and it has enabled him to find positions that he enjoys and use his understanding of brand to recruit, find and hire great employees.

Brand YOU

Kraig Brown

Kraig Brown

Brand Billboard™: A leader in sales excellence, seasoned sales innovator bringing revolution to sales
Occupation: Vice President of Sales
Twitter: kraigrbrown
LinkedIn: http://www.linkedin.com/in/kraigrbrown
Blog: http://www.kraigbrown.wordpress.com/

Think sales genius, think amazing results and the ability to lead teams and develop great leaders, and you will be spot on with the brand that Kraig Brown has developed. He has worked to brand himself as a sales innovator, developing the next generation of sales tools using advanced video technology.

He incorporates work life balance into the equation, and sees that the biggest impact that mobile technology and social media has is the stretch of the 8-5 paradigm and the desegmentation of our lives, ultimately making us more human with greater productivity. Kraig Brown is sales revolution.

It is not just his 60+ references listed on LinkedIn that makes him stand out. It is a combination proven results time and time again as evidence by great descriptors and write-ups, a Twitter profile with more than 11,000 followers, and being a sales leader that has learned how to combine performance and a great brand.

Marc Cenedella

Marc Cenedella

Brand Billboard™:   Widely recognized thought leader
on job search, career management, recruiting and business
Occupation: Founder and CEO of TheLadders.com
Twitter: cenedella
Blog: http://www.cenedella.com/job-search/the-boy-who-followed-somebody-elses-dream/
LinkedIn: http://www.linkedin.com/in/cenedella
Company website: http://www.TheLadders.com

Marc Cenedella is the CEO and Founder of
TheLadders.com, the world's largest professional jobs
website.

Marc is on record saying, "It's the recognition that living in
society with people, your success is as dependent on what
others think about what you can do as it is on what **you** can
actually do." Marc and his team understand personal
branding. They work to build brands for job seekers that
find them positions and secure for them a better future.
TheLadders.com focuses on job seekers in the over
$100,000 a year category.

Mark himself is a branding genius. He runs a blog,
regularly communicates with a large job seeker audience,
takes his show on the road to meet his customers, and
continually updates the tools and help that the site offers
job seekers around the globe.

Brand **YOU**

Marc has created a useful and amazing site, while understanding both the impact of the brand of the site, his personal brand, and the impact that personal branding has on every job seeker that visits his web site. Marc and team have done a great job espousing the benefits of personal branding and working to educate job seekers on improving their own personal brands. We can learn not only from their example, but also from the many tools available on his web site. Thanks, Marc, for an incredible resource and site.

He has started a 'Signature' program that guarantees a job, for a minimal fee, or your money back after six months. And what do they do to help? They develop your brand, re-write your resume, help you with connections, and create an opportunity and, ultimately, a job for you.

Wayne O'Neill

> # Wayne O'Neill
>
> **Brand Billboard™:** Dynamic business developer, reshaping the way organizations develop and win business
> **Occupation:** CEO
> **Blog:**
> http://www.wayneoneill.typepad.com/changing_the_game_connect/
> **LinkedIn:** http://www.linkedin.com/in/wayneoneill
> **Company website:** http://www.woassociates.com/

Wayne is a dynamic business developer. He knows what it takes to build a sustainable business development capability, and he uses that in both his brand and the work that he does day to day. He believes that key elements, client intelligence, teamwork and connecting combine to create amazing business-development results. His brand has created success for him both personally and professionally. He uses his brand and skills to help organizations move faster in account development.

Wayne's brand comes across in his messaging. It is fresh, new, out-of-the-box text and graphics that get YOU thinking a different way. Wayne is out-of-the-box. His brand is a stark contrast to the "We can't get to it," "It won't work," and "It will take a lot of time and money" messages that exist in many of the organizations that he has worked with. He is about relationships. He is about client intelligence. He is about making sustainable changes in organizations that create game-changing strategies.

He is writing a book titled *The Rich Get Richer...and the Poor Keep Submitting Proposals* and is a shining example of a brand giant. Wayne gets personal branding.

You have come to the end of your branding journey. I hope that you have found helpful information that will assist you in your career path. Knowledge, combined with action will create results that will shine a light on your path.

I wish for you a fruitful and enjoyable journey. Best wishes.

The End

Brand YOU

Personal Brand "To Do" List Summary

Chapter 1: Why Do You Need This?
○ Locate five people to assess your work and what YOU stand for

○ Evaluate YOUR view of your work

○ Identify your strengths

Chapter 2: How to Define Your Brand
○ Identify what you want to be known for

○ Document your strengths

○ Write out the top three characteristics reflected in your proudest accomplishments

○ Write out three desired characteristics for your desired or current role

○ Create a logo and a catch phrase

Chapter 3: Creating Your Brand
○ Create a message for your brand

○ Write or update your biography

○ Begin to think about communicating your brand

○ Re-tool your image

Chapter 4: The Cornerstones of your brand
○ What values do you stand for?

○ Incorporate these into your brand

○ Be sure that you are true to yourself

○ Think about your maximum potential

Chapter 5: Advertising Your Brand

O Determine how you will advertise your brand

O Make a plan to promote yourself through email

O Create a list of "targets": people to whom you'd like to communicate your brand message

Chapter 6: The Google Effect

O Google yourself

O Make yourself 'findable'

O Claim internet sources for yourself, i.e. www.spokeo.com

O Set up Google alerts

Chapter 7: LinkedIn & Plaxo

O Create a LinkedIn profile at www.linkedin.com

O Check out Plaxo www.plaxo.com

O Continue to enhance your LinkedIn profile, finding examples that you like

Chapter 8: Facebook & Twitter

O Create a Facebook account at www.facebook.com

O Check out Twitter at www.twitter.com

Chapter 9: HootSuite & Tweetdeck

O Evaluate the advantage of HootSuite, www.hootsuite.com, and Tweetdeck , www.tweetdeck.com

O Plot on your calendar regular intervals to network/touch base with contacts in your network

Chapter 10: Be Unique

○ Re-evaluate: Have you created a brand that is different enough to stand out in a crowded marketplace?

○ Celebrate what makes you different

○ Find and use your passions

Chapter 11: Hall of Famers

○ Write out your brand, your messaging plan, and your action items

○ Annually or bi-annually review your plan

Congratulations on completing the branding journey!

Good luck,

Bethany Williams

Connect with the author via
http://www.BethanyWilliams.org